DK EYEW

W9-AHY-285

TOP **10**
SCOTLAND

Top 10 Scotland Highlights

The Top 10 of Everything

CONTENTS

Scotland Area by Area

Streetsmart

Within each Top 10 list in this book, no hierarchy of quality or popularity is implied. All 10 are, in the editor's opinion, of roughly equal merit.

Title page, front cover and spine *The majestic ruins of Kilchurne Castle across Loch Awe*
Back cover, clockwise from top left *Jacobite Steam Train at Glenfinnan; Isle of Harris; University of Glasgow; Calton Hill, Edinburgh*

Welcome to
Scotland

Shimmering lochs, silent glens, romantic castles, remote islands, riotous festivals, drams of whisky and rounds of golf. The birthplace of "Rabbie" Burns and Harry Potter is a proud nation, and no wonder: Scotland has fuelled the passions of artists, writers and adventurers for centuries. With Eyewitness Top 10 Scotland, it's your turn to be inspired.

It may be small, but few countries can match Scotland's mix of scenic splendour and cultural heritage. What could be more romantic than crossing the sea to the **Isle of Skye**, more moving than seeing the site of the **Glencoe** massacre or more exciting than joining the crowds thronging the streets during the world-famous **Edinburgh International Festival**? And what could be more thrilling than watching ospreys in the **Cairngorms National Park**, monster-spotting for "Nessie" on **Loch Ness**, or exploring fairy-tale **Glamis Castle** – supposedly one of the most haunted places in Britain?

Scotland has long attracted thrill-seekers, who come to "bag" a Munro or to hike the **West Highland Way**. Yet its gentler activities are prized too, such as dolphin-spotting on the Moray Firth or strolling amongst the exotic plants of **Inverewe Gardens**. Its cultural attractions are equally varied: Impressionist paintings and Dolly the Sheep in Glasgow; Edinburgh's museums and galleries; Victorian industry in **New Lanark's** historic streets and Viking graffiti at **Maeshowe** on Orkney.

Whether you're visiting for a weekend or a week, our Top 10 guide brings together the best of everything Scotland has to offer, from mysterious **Rosslyn Chapel** to mighty **Edinburgh Castle**. The guide has useful tips throughout, from seeking out what's free to avoiding the crowds, plus 11 easy-to-follow itineraries, designed to tie together a clutch of sights in a short space of time. Add inspiring photography and detailed maps, and you've got the essential pocket-sized travel companion. **Enjoy the book, and enjoy Scotland**.

Clockwise from top: **Portree harbour in Skye, Scottish dancers, Greyfriars Bobby in Edinburgh, Rua Reidh Lighthouse near Gairloch on the northwest coast, the Falkirk Wheel, Highland cattle, Scottish Parliament in Edinburgh**

Exploring Scotland

Scotland boasts wild landscapes, ancient castles and bustling cities. To help make the most of your stay and get a flavour for this fascinating country, here are ideas for a two-day and a seven-day Scottish jaunt.

The Queen's Gallery, at the Palace of Holyroodhouse, exhibits works from the Royal Collection.

Forth Bridge, a UNESCO World Heritage Site, is a cantilever railway bridge near Edinburgh.

Two Days in Scotland

Day ❶
MORNING
Start in Edinburgh with the historic **Royal Mile** (see pp14–15) and tour the Palace of Holyroodhouse.

AFTERNOON
Choose between the **National Museum of Scotland** (see pp18–19) or the **Scottish National Gallery** (see pp16–17). Wander to elegant New Town to shop at **Jenners** (see p79), then take in the fabulous city views from **Calton Hill** (see p76).

Day ❷
MORNING
Drive to romantic **Linlithgow Palace** (see p86), then continue to the site of the battle of **Bannockburn** (see p103).

AFTERNOON
Take in dramatic **Stirling Castle** (see p103) and visit the Wallace Monument. Return via the charming streets of **Culross** (see p91) and majestic **Forth Bridge** (see p94).

Key
— Two-day itinerary
— Seven-day itinerary

Seven Days in Scotland

Day ❶
As day 1 of Two Days in Scotland.

Day ❷
MORNING
Cross the Forth to visit historic **Scone Palace** (see p92) before lunching by the silvery Tay in Perth.

AFTERNOON
Head for Loch of the Lowes, near **Dunkeld** (see p94), to view the ospreys (Apr–Aug). Then continue through Pitlochry to the picturesque gorge at Killiecrankie.

Day ❸
MORNING
Ride the UK's highest funicular railway up **Cairngorm** (see p35), then warm your cockles at a distillery on Speyside's Malt Whisky Trail.

Eilean Donan Castle is one of Scotland's iconic sites, located on an island where three lochs converge.

AFTERNOON

Spot **Moray Firth dolphins** (see p112) from the shore of Spey Bay. Overnight in Highlands city **Inverness** (see p117).

Day **4**
MORNING

Explore the bleak **Culloden Battlefield** (see p117), then keep your eyes peeled on a "monster" cruise on the famous Loch Ness.

AFTERNOON

Watch boats on the Caledonian canal at **Fort Augustus** (see p29). Bear west to **Eilean Donan Castle** (see p118), then cross the bridge from Kyle of Lochalsh to **Isle of Skye** (see pp26–7).

Day **5**
MORNING

Start early and visit **Dunvegan Castle** (see p26), ancestral home of the Clan Macleod and purportedly the oldest inhabited castle of Scotland.

AFTERNOON

Take a boat trip from Elgol to **Loch Coruisk** (see p26). Leave the Isle of Skye from Armadale in time to catch the last ferry to Mallaig (summer: 6:40pm).

Day **6**
MORNING

Admire the **Glenfinnan Monument** (see p118) and viaduct, and continue to sombre **Glencoe** (see pp30–31).

AFTERNOON

Take the High Road to **Loch Lomond** (see p103), stopping in pretty Luss for a break, and arriving in **Glasgow** (see pp96–101) in time for dinner.

Day **7**
MORNING

Spend the morning at **Kelvingrove Art Gallery and Museum** (see pp20–21) or the **Riverside Museum** (see pp22–3).

AFTERNOON

Down the Ayrshire coast find **Culzean Castle** (see pp32–3) and the **Robert Burns Birthplace Museum** (see p85).

Top 10 Scotland Highlights

Rib-vaulted ceiling and stained-glass windows
of St Giles' Cathedral, Edinburgh

TOP10 Scotland Highlights

Scotland has an overwhelming abundance of natural beauty; hundreds of castles stand proud from its long and turbulent past, and an innate flair for enterprise and travel has endowed the nation with artistic treasures from around the world. The culture remains vibrant today, and there's much to celebrate. Here's a distillation of Scotland's best.

Edinburgh Castle ①

Presiding over the nation's capital, the castle is Scotland's pre-eminent sight, a truly inspirational historical and cultural landmark (see pp12–13).

② Scottish National Gallery

The gallery's internationally significant collection ranges from early Renaissance masterpieces to works by Rembrandt, Ramsay and Raeburn (see pp16–17).

③ National Museum of Scotland

The main museum has one of Scotland's great eclectic collections. The modern wing takes on Scotland from prehistory to the 20th century (see pp18–19).

Kelvingrove Art Gallery and Museum ④

Inside its grand Spanish Baroque-style shell, Scotland's premier museum and art gallery houses one of Europe's great civic art collections (see pp20–21).

⑤ Riverside Museum

This is one of Glasgow's major museums, and has a spellbinding array of interactive exhibits, visual enthralment as well as stimulation aplenty across all things transport and leisure. It is impossible not to be wowed by the numerous wonders it has to offer (see pp22–3).

Port of Ness
Kinlochbervie
Stornoway
Seisiadar
Scourie
Isle of Lewis
The Minch
Ledmore
Tarbert
Gairloch
Uig
Shieldaig
Dunvegan
Raasay
North
Isle of Skye ⑥
Broadford
Elgol
Loch Morar
Mallaig
Fort William
Kilchoan
Glencoe ⑧
Coll
Dervaig
Tiree
Scarnish
Isle of Mull
Oban
Iona
Inveraray
Atlantic Ocean
Kilmartin
Port Askaig
Jura
Tarbert
Dunmore
Islay
Portnahaven
Gigha
Brodick
Port Ellen
Arran
Campbeltown
Culzean Castle ⑨
North Channel
Cairnryan
Drummore

6 Isle of Skye
Skye is an island of romantic tales and the pursuit of royalty, of strange landscapes and formidable mountain ranges, of castle strongholds and religious communities (see pp26–7).

Loch Ness and the Great Glen 7
The Great Glen is Scotland's deepest cut, a swath that splits the land in two. A course of water runs through this great valley, forming notorious Loch Ness (see pp28–9).

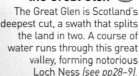

8 Glencoe
Described by Dickens as the "burial ground of a race of giants", there is indeed something ominous about this raw terrain, site of a 1692 massacre (see pp30–31).

9 Culzean Castle
The castle stands proud on a windswept clifftop, but Culzean is a velvet hand in an iron glove; inside is given over to Robert Adam's play on the rules of Classicism (see pp32–3).

The Cairngorms 10
This region offers truly spectacular views. Bird lovers, walkers and winter sports enthusiasts praying for snow all head to the woodlands, rivers, lochs and mountains of the Cairngorms, the highest landmass in Great Britain. From ospreys to Arctic flowers, it's all here to discover (see pp34–5).

Map labels:
Durness, Tongue, Thurso, Thurso, Wick, Lybster, Helmsdale, Lairg, Golspie, North Sea, West Highlands, Garve, Nairn, Moray Firth, Elgin, Portsoy, Fraserburgh, Keith, Peterhead, Inverness, Huntly, 7 Loch Ness Great Glen, Grantown-on-Spey, Inverurie, Aberdeen, Laggan, 10 The Cairngorms, Stonehaven, Grampian Mountains, Brechin, St. Cyrus, Pitlochry, Forfar, Arbroath, Dundee, Perth, North Sea, Callander, Cupar, Crail, Stirling, Firth of Forth, 4 5, Edinburgh, 1 2 3, Glasgow, Peebles, Cumnock, Southern Uplands, Jedburgh, Loch Trool, Moffat, Teviothead, Newton Stewart, Dumfries, Gatehouse of Fleet

0 km 40
0 miles 40

Edinburgh Castle

Dominating the city's skyline since the 12th century, this castle is a national icon and, deservedly, one of the country's most popular visitor attractions. Din Eidyn, "the stronghold of Eidyn", from which Edinburgh takes its name, was the vital possession in Scotland's wars. Varying roles as royal palace, barracks, prison and parliament have all helped shape this castle, home to the Scottish crown jewels and the fabled Stone of Destiny.

1 Gatehouse and Portcullis Gate

The gatehouse was built in 1886–8 more for its looks than functionality. The two bronze statues are of William Wallace and Robert the Bruce (see p103). The original entrance was via the formidable Portcullis Gate of around 1574.

2 Great Hall

The outstanding feature of this hall (below) is the hammer-beam roof supported on projecting stone corbels. Take time to study all the enchanting little carvings. Constructed around 1500, this is Scotland's oldest wooden roof and probably its most magnificent.

The imposing façade of Edinburgh Castle

3 Argyle Battery

The castle's northern defence offers spectacular views. Don't miss the One O'Clock Gun, fired here every day except Sunday from a great 25-pounder cannon.

4 Crown Jewels and the Stone of Destiny

The UK's oldest crown jewels have lain here since about 1615. However, the fabled Stone of Destiny has been here only since 1996.

5 Scottish National War Memorial

The National War Memorial (right) lists all of Scotland's war dead since 1914. Exterior carvings include a phoenix, symbol of the surviving spirit.

7 St Margaret's Chapel

This tiny, charmingly simple building is the oldest structure surviving from the medieval castle. Probably built by David I (1124–53) in honour of his sanctified mother, it is still used today, and contains some wonderful stained glass **(left)**.

8 Royal Palace

Here in 1566, in a small panelled chamber, Mary Queen of Scots gave birth to James VI, the first king to rule both Scotland and England.

9 Governor's House

This elegant house is beautifully proportioned. It can only be viewed from the outside, as it is still reserved for ceremonial use.

10 Mons Meg

A cannon **(below)** of awesome proportions now sits outside St Margaret's Chapel. Built in Belgium in 1449, it could fire a 150-kg (330-lb) stone ball over 2 miles (3.5 km) – cutting-edge technology in the Middle Ages.

6 Prison Vaults

During the 18th and 19th centuries, the castle's vaults were used to hold French prisoners of war. Their graffiti can still be seen, as can the objects they made, such as bone dyes for forging banknotes.

Plan of the Castle

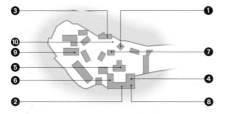

STONE OF DESTINY

According to the mythology that surrounds the Stone, this is the very rock that Jacob used as a pillow when he dreamed of angels ascending to heaven (Genesis 28). For centuries it was kept in Scone Palace, near Perth (see p92), and used as the coronation throne for Scottish kings until Edward I invaded in 1296 and carried the Stone back to England. For 700 years it was kept under the throne in Westminster Abbey, until it was returned to Scotland in 1996.

NEED TO KNOW

MAP M4 ■ Castle Hill, Edinburgh, EH1 2NG
■ (0131) 225 9846
■ www.edinburgh
castle.scot

Open Apr–Sep: 9:30am–6pm daily (Oct–Mar: to 5pm) ; last adm 1 hour before closing; closed Christmas Day & Boxing Day; tours every 30 min

Adm £19.50; concessions £16; children £11.50

■ Book tickets online for reduced prices and guaranteed entry time.

■ The official tours are witty and informative. You can also take a multilingual audio tour, proceeding in whatever order takes your fancy.

■ Although a large variety of food can be found on the Royal Mile just outside the castle, choice at the castle itself is limited to either the Tea Rooms or the Redcoat Café (see p77).

The Royal Mile

John Knox's House on Edinburgh's Royal Mile

1 John Knox's House
MAP P3 ■ 43–5 High St ■ (0131) 556 9579 ■ Open 10am–6pm Mon–Sat (Jul & Aug: from noon Sun) ■ Adm ■ www.scottishstorytellingcentre.com

The best-known little house in Edinburgh, with its quaint steps up from the street, is now part of the Scottish Storytelling Centre. It was the home of Scotland's fiery religious reformer, John Knox, in 1599. Worth squeezing into for its antiquity alone.

2 Writers' Museum
MAP N3 ■ Lady Stair's Close ■ (0131) 529 4901 ■ Open 10am–5pm daily ■ www.edinburgh museums.org.uk

Occupying Lady Stair's House (built in 1622), and set in a charming court-yard, this is the place (see p78) to learn about the three great Scottish writers, Robert Burns, Sir Walter Scott and Robert Louis Stevenson, through portraits, manuscripts and personal possessions (see p78).

3 St Giles' Cathedral
MAP N4 ■ High St ■ (0131) 225 9442 ■ Open May–Sep: 9am–7pm Mon–Fri (to 5pm Sat), 1–5pm Sun; Oct–Apr: 9am–5pm daily ■ Donation ■ www.stgilescathedral.org.uk

This building (see p78) has been a landmark and a marvel since 1160. Look for the bagpiping angel (near entrance), the exhilarating rib-vaulted ceiling of the Thistle Chapel and those ancient tatty flags. There is a self-service café and a shop here as well.

4 Scottish Storytelling Centre
MAP P3 ■ 43–5 High St ■ (0131) 556 9579 ■ Open 10am–6pm Mon–Sat (Jul & Aug: from noon Sun) ■ www.scottishstorytellingcentre.com

A theatre with a wide range of entertainment, but the insider thing to do here is enquire about the local storytellers. They hold meetings in the café on the last Friday of every month, where anyone can enjoy the craic (good times). Nothing flamboyant, but real local culture.

THE ROYAL MILE

The city's most historic street formed the main thoroughfare of medieval Edinburgh, linking the castle to Holyroodhouse. Congested with street performers during the Festival (see p68), it is a hub of activity and entertainment year-round. Don't miss the narrow closes off the main street.

5 Museum of Childhood

MAP P3 ▪ 42 High St ▪ (0131) 529 4142 ▪ Open 10am–5pm daily ▪ www.edinburghmuseums.org.uk

Teddy bears, rocking horses, toy soldiers and castor oil – childhood memories come rippling back in the minds of adult visitors. But today's children find the Museum of Childhood just as enthralling, as they discover what amused the "oldies" long ago. New exhibits include a Buzz Lightyear action figure.

6 Historic and Ghostly Tours

Mercat Tours: (0131) 225 5445; www.mercattours.com ▪ Auld Reekie Tours: (0131) 557 4700; www.auldreekietours.com ▪ Cadies & Witchery Tours: (0131) 225 6745; www.witchery tours.com ▪ City of Edinburgh Tours: (0131) 220 6868; www. cityofedinburghtours.com

A fascinating tour can be taken of Mary King's Close *(see p78)*, a medieval street sealed up in 1646 after its inhabitants died of the plague. Alternatively, choose an adrenalin-pumping ghost tour – evenings are best.

The Witchery Tour

7 Scottish Parliament

MAP R3 ▪ Canongate ▪ (0131) 348 5200 ▪ Open 10am–5pm Mon–Sat, public hols & all days Parliament is in recess ▪ www.parliament.scot

Spanish architect Enric Mirrales's controversial design of "upturned boats" won the competition for a landmark building for the new Scottish Parliament. Higher up the Mile is the old Parliament House.

8 Museum of Edinburgh

MAP Q3 ▪ 142 Canongate ▪ (0131) 529 4143 ▪ Open 10am–5pm daily ▪ www.edinburgh museums.org.uk

A medieval house, this museum has a specialist local collection. A maze of rooms comprises primitive axe heads, Roman coins and all manner of historical finds gathered from the street since the Neolithic Age.

Map of the Royal Mile

9 The Palace of Holyroodhouse

MAP R3 ▪ Royal Mile ▪ (0303) 123 7306 ▪ Open Apr–Oct: 9:30am–6pm daily (Nov–Mar: to 4:30pm daily); last adm 1 hour before closing (call to check for closing times) ▪ Adm ▪ www. royalcollection.org.uk

The royal residence *(see p76)* was known for love and murder in the time of Mary Queen of Scots. The state rooms are used by the current Queen. Climb nearby Arthur's Seat in Holyrood Park for views.

10 Camera Obscura

MAP M4 ▪ Castlehill ▪ (0131) 226 3709 ▪ Open Apr–Jun: 9:30am–8pm daily; Jul & Aug: 9:30am–10pm daily; Sep & Oct: 9:30am–8pm Sun–Fri (to 9pm Sat); Nov–Mar: 9:30am–7pm Mon–Thu (to 8pm Fri & Sun, 9pm Sat) ▪ Adm ▪ www.camera-obscura.co.uk

This historic observatory has a roving mirror that projects a 360° panorama of Edinburgh, so it is a great place to start exploring the city. It also drops you into a world of illusion and warped images to startling effect.

The vortex tunnel at Camera Obscura

TOP 10 ⭐ Scottish National Gallery

A striking Neo-Classical building midway along Edinburgh's Princes Street, the National Gallery defies you to miss it and is widely regarded as one of the finest smaller galleries in the world. The collection is a manageable concentration of excellence, including works by the greatest names in Western art – Raphael, Titian, El Greco, Rembrandt, and Monet, to name but a few – as well as a comprehensive array of Scottish masterpieces. The museum is being redeveloped until 2021, so phone ahead to check open galleries during that time.

① Seven Sacraments
The seven works depicting the rites of Christianity evoke grand theatricality; they are considered the finest pieces by Nicolas Poussin, founder of French Classical painting.

② An Old Woman Cooking Eggs
Velázquez's creation of mood through strong contrast was unprecedented in Spain when he produced this startling work **(below)** in 1618.

③ Lady Agnew of Lochnaw
The lady's languid pose and direct gaze in this portrait **(above)** caused a stir in 1892, launching her as a society beauty and giving John Singer Sargent cult status among Edwardian-era portrait painters.

④ The Virgin Adoring the Sleeping Christ Child
The painting's brilliant range of tones has now been revealed following careful restoration. An unusual Botticelli work for having been painted on canvas and not wood.

⑤ Rev Robert Walker Skating on Duddingston Loch
One of the most celebrated paintings by a Scottish painter, the fun-loving minister depicted by Henry Raeburn is known to have been a member of the prestigious Edinburgh Skating Club.

⑥ Dutch Collection
The pick of the best from the Dutch collection must include Rembrandt's world-weary *Self-Portrait Aged 51*, though *A Woman in Bed* also has an impressive depth of character. Dutch paintings in the galleries include works by Frans Hals, such as his lively, naturalistic *Portrait of Verdonck*.

7 Italian Renaissance Paintings

Works by Leonardo da Vinci and Raphael stand out here. Leonardo's *Madonna of the Yarnwinder* depicts the Christ child holding a spindle shaped like a cross, while Titian's *The Three Ages of Man* reminds us of everlasting love.

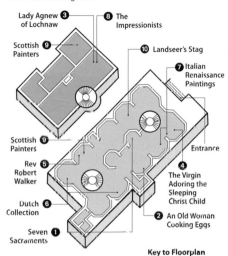

Lady Agnew of Lochnaw 3
The Impressionists 8
Scottish Painters 9
Landseer's Stag 10
Italian Renaissance Paintings 7
Scottish Painters 9
Entrance
Rev Robert Walker 5
Dutch Collection 6
The Virgin Adoring the Sleeping Christ Child 4
An Old Woman Cooking Eggs 2
Seven Sacraments 1

Floorplan of Scottish National Gallery

Key to Floorplan
■ Upper floor
■ Ground floor

8 The Impressionists

You can find works by Impressionists such as Monet and Cezanne here, as well as Gauguin's *Vision of the Sermon* (Jacob Wrestling with the Angel) and Van Gogh's *Orchard in Blossom* **(below)**.

9 Scottish Painters

The collection includes superb portraits by Ramsay, Raeburn and Guthrie, *Pitlessie Fair* by Sir David Wilkie aged 16, and *Saint Bride* by John Duncan. Check to see which works are being displayed during restoration.

10 Landseer's Stag

Sir Edwin Landseer's *Monarch of the Glen* is known to be one of the most famous of all Victorian British paintings. It depicts a magnificent stag in a Highland setting.

TOP 10 ⭐ National Museum of Scotland

The best and rarest of Scotland's antiquities have been brought together in this treasure trove occupying connected buildings on Edinburgh's Chambers Street. Both buildings maintain separate identities: the older 19th-century building concentrates on international artifacts, while the modern sandstone wing is dedicated to the story of Scotland and its people.

1 Lewis Chess Pieces

These enchanting ivory figures – an anxious king, a pious bishop, glum warriors – were made by Viking invaders in the 12th century.

2 Monymusk Reliquary

Reliquaries were containers used for storing holy relics. The Monymusk Reliquary is connected to St Columba and Robert the Bruce, hero of Bannockburn *(see p38)*. It dates back to the 8th century and, although it's tiny, the craftsmanship is exceptional. It is one of the museum's most prized possessions.

3 The Maiden

This is a grisly relic to put a shiver down your spine. The Maiden was a Scottish beheading machine, which predated the French guillotine, with a weighted blade that descended from on high. It was used to behead more than 150 of those condemned in Edinburgh between 1564 and 1710, including its inventor.

Display of Vivienne Westwood's tartan suit

4 Art, Design and Fashion

Opened in 2016, this gallery showcases innovation in applied arts, fashion and design. Among the many exhibits, the most eye-catching are six Wedgwood plates by Sir Eduardo Paolozzi from the 1970s and a tartan suit by Vivienne Westwood (1993).

5 Bonnie Prince Charlie's Canteen

Find the fugitive Prince's *(see p27)* cutlery, corkscrew, bottles, cup and condiments set here, and picture him in the wild with his lustrous travelling canteen.

6 Ancient Egypt Rediscovered

Covering more than 4,000 years of Egyptian history, this gallery showcases iconic objects **(left)** from this ancient culture. Exhibits include a complete royal burial group as well as exquisite gold jewellery.

7 Natural History

Dinosaur skeletons and stuffed animals cascade down from the ceiling, producing spectacular visual results that almost bring them to life.

8 Dolly the Sheep

An ordinary-looking sheep **(left)** that's anything but that. As the world's first cloned mammal, Dolly was a scientific marvel.

The Buildings 9

The National Museum first opened as the Royal Museum in 1866 and has been a city landmark ever since. Its cavernous interior and marvellous roof create an extraordinary feeling of light and space. The sandstone wing **(right)** has been heralded as one of the most important constructions in post-war Scotland.

Floorplan of National Museum of Scotland

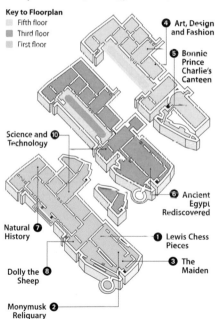

Key to Floorplan
- Fifth floor
- Third floor
- First floor

4 Art, Design and Fashion

5 Bonnie Prince Charlie's Canteen

Science and Technology 10

6 Ancient Egypt Rediscovered

Natural History 7

1 Lewis Chess Pieces

Dolly the Sheep 8

3 The Maiden

Monymusk Reliquary 2

ORIENTATION

Centred on the vast foyer, the older part of the National Museum is spread over three floors. Wandering the many halls can be confusing, so pick up a floor plan or ask the staff for help. The layout of the sandstone wing, accessed by the Tower Entrance, is more straightforward. The roof terrace of the Scottish Galleries offers spectacular views of the city.

NEED TO KNOW

MAP N4 Chambers St, Edinburgh, EH1 1JF
(0300) 123 6789
www.nms.ac.uk

Open 10am–5pm daily

There are temporary exhibits on display thoughout the year.

Check timings and schedule for free guided tours at the main desk.

The museum's rooftop Tower Restaurant has fantastic views.

10 Science and Technology

Dolly the Sheep is just one of Scotland's modern scientific achievements. This gallery looks at some of the country's other genetic research along with its Nobel Prize-winning work on pharmaceuticals. One particularly futuristic exhibit looks at the production of state-of-the-art body implants and prosthetic limbs, developed by local company Touch Bionics.

⬛10 ⭐ Kelvingrove Art Gallery and Museum

Scotland's most visited collection comprises some 8,000 works of international significance. The collection takes in worldwide ancient cultures, as well as European and Scottish art across the centuries, and provides insights into the development of Glasgow from medieval times through to its cultural transformation in the 19th to 21st centuries, including the 2014 Commonwealth Games, when the city stole the show with its hospitality and sense of fun. There is also a quirky playfulness in Kelvingrove's contrasting displays.

1 Miss Cranston's Tearoom

Between 1900 and 1921 the venerable Charles Rennie Mackintosh (1868–1928) was the sole designer for Catherine Cranston's tearoom empire. These beautiful interiors are of both artistic and social significance.

2 Ceremonial Turtle Posts

These striking posts were sent to Glasgow from the Torres Straits Islands, off Australia, by a Scottish missionary in 1889 and are the only surviving examples in the world. Decorated with feathers and carvings, they conjure up mystical Islander celebrations.

West Court, Kelvingrove Art Gallery and Museum

3 Spitfire

The Spitfire LA198, 602 City of Glasgow Squadron, hangs dramatically from the ceiling of the West Court **(above)**, soaring above the bodies of stuffed giraffes and wild cats. It is recognized as the best-restored warplane of its kind in the UK.

4 Old Willie the Village Worthy

A leading figure in the group of young, rebellious Scottish artists known as the Glasgow Boys, James Guthrie (1859–1930) produced internationally significant work in the late 19th century. The unsentimental *Old Willie the Village Worthy* **(left)**, is one of Guthrie's finest realist portraits.

5 A Man in Armour

This fine painting by Rembrandt, considered by many the greatest artist of the Dutch Golden Age, is a bold depiction of a young man, probably Alexander the Great, weighed down by his armour. Kelvingrove curators voted it their favourite piece. The work dates back to the mid-17th century.

6 Paddle Canoe

This fascinating paddle canoe, which was carved from a single piece of wood, is one of the few remaining artifacts from a forgotten world. It dates back to Scotland's Bronze Age (c.2500–800 BC) and would have been used by early people living in crannogs, or loch dwellings.

Floorplan of Kelvingrove Art Gallery and Museum

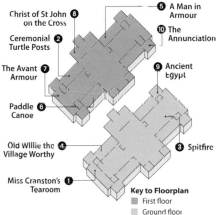

- 8 Christ of St John on the Cross
- 2 Ceremonial Turtle Posts
- 7 The Avant Armour
- 6 Paddle Canoe
- 4 Old Willie the Village Worthy
- 1 Miss Cranston's Tearoom
- 5 A Man in Armour
- 10 The Annunciation
- 9 Ancient Egypt
- 3 Spitfire

Key to Floorplan
■ First floor
■ Ground floor

7 The Avant Armour

This artwork and tool of war is one of the oldest near-complete suits of armour in the world and is still in almost perfect condition. Made in Milan, a centre of armour-making, in around 1440, it is a key piece in Kelvingrove's collection.

8 Christ of St John on the Cross

Salvador Dalí's surrealist painting was first displayed in 1952. The unusual angle of the Crucifixion attracted admiration, criticism and controversy, which was typical of Dalí.

9 Ancient Egypt

Wonders abound in the Ancient Egypt gallery, including the obligatory mummies and tombs. The coffin and mummy of Egyptian lady Ankhesnefer date back to 610 BC. Her mummified body has remained undisturbed since her funeral and burial approximately 2,500 years ago.

10 The Annunciation

This intimate work (**left**) by Italian master painter Sandro Botticelli (1445–1510) was probably commissioned for a private patron and used for prayer and meditation. The fine detail in the work is embellished with the use of real gold for rays of light, representing God's grace.

MUSEUM GUIDE

The main collections and galleries are set out on the ground and first floors. Highlights on the ground floor are the excellent Scottish Art and Design galleries, while on the first floor the Dutch and Italian collections are particularly fine. On the lower ground floor there is a temporary gallery space reserved for major touring exhibitions, the restaurant and the main gift shop.

NEED TO KNOW

MAP Y2 ■ Argyle St, Glasgow G3 8AG
■ (0141) 276 9599
■ www.glasgowlife.org.uk/museums/kelvingrove

Open 10am–5pm Mon–Thu & Sat (from 11am Fri & Sun)

■ Check the information desk for details of special events and talks.

■ Head downstairs to the Kelvingrove Cafe for table service and a range of snacks and main courses. Or cross over the road to Firebird, a child-friendly café serving wood-fired pizzas and more.

■ Take a stroll through nearby Kelvingrove Park to visit the small Hunterian Museum and Art Gallery.

TOP 10 ⭐ Riverside Museum

This stunning £74 million museum sits on the banks of the Clyde and is devoted to transport and leisure. Its 3,000 fascinating items range from horse-drawn vehicles and police cars to Stanley Spencer murals and skateboards. There's a dress that was worn by Audrey Hepburn and the motorbike Ewan McGregor rode around the world. Climb aboard a tram or stand on the footplate of a historic locomotive. There are interactive displays, films and images and, moored on the quay, a 19th-century sailing ship.

1 The Building
Take time after to stroll around outside and take in award-winning Iraqi architect Zaha Hadid's building **(above)**, which sits on the Clyde on the site of a former shipyard. The jagged roof is striking, and the interior is free of supports to accommodate the many large exhibits.

2 South African Locomotive
Built in Glasgow in 1945, this enormous locomotive spent more than 40 years crossing South Africa. It is the largest object in the collection and one of a number of restored trains.

3 All Things Bike
Bicycles and motorbikes on display include Danny MacAskill's stunt bicycle, homemade bikes and the world's oldest pedal bike. Suspended from the ceiling is a model velodrome.

4 Recreated Streets
There are three recreated streets that take you back to the Glasgow of the past. Most atmospheric is the cobbled 19th-century street with its shops, pub and an interactive photographer's studio.

THE CLYDE

"Glasgow made the Clyde and the Clyde made Glasgow." After trade in sugar and tobacco expanded in the 18th century, engineers deepened the Clyde, which eventually allowed boats to dock in the city itself, rather than unload their cargoes downriver. International trade flourished, shipbuilding became a major industry and Glasgow grew into the "second city" of the British empire.

Floorplan of Riverside Museum

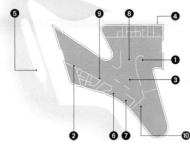

NEED TO KNOW

MAP Y2 ■ 100 Pointhouse Place, Glasgow G3 8RS
■ (0141) 287 2720
■ www.glasgowlife. org.uk/museums/ riverside

Open 10am–5pm Mon–Thu & Sat (from 11am Fri & Sun)

The Tall Ship: Pointhouse Quay; (0141) 357 3699; open 10am–4pm daily

■ The café on the ground floor has great views of the Clyde; in warmer weather you can dine outside on the terrace.

■ There are free guided tours on most days and fun family quiz sheets. Ask at the reception.

5 The Tall Ship

Moored on the Clyde outside the museum, the *Glenlee* **(right)** is one of only five Clyde-built sailing ships that remain afloat. Built in the 19th century, she circumnavigated the globe four times. Go on board and tour the ship; you can even see the captain's cabin.

6 The Italian Café

Glasgow's Italian community has been well established in the city since the 19th century. They make great ice cream and have founded a number of much-loved cafés in the city and along the Ayrshire coast. Visit this re-created 1930s café to experience those halcyon days.

8 Glasgow Tram

Glasgow's trams achieved iconic status and were an important part of the city's culture until 1962. You can step inside this original street-car **(right)** and discover stories associated with the trams and city life.

7 The Subway

Step into a model section of the Glasgow subway and climb into a carriage from an old underground train. You can watch a World War II drama unfold, with evacuated children and soldiers boarding the trains.

9 Vintage Cars

There aren't many places where you can see the first Hillman Imp, an Argyll motor as well as a pristine Strathclyde Police Ford Granada. A wide variety of old and new cars **(left)** are on display here. Many are reminders of Glasgow's famous motor industry.

10 Clyde-Built Ships

Glasgow was once a world-famous centre of shipbuilding and the museum has 159 superb models of Clyde-built ships, including luxury liners and warships. Models include the *Cutty Sark*, the *Lusitania* and the *Queen Mary*. There is also a World War I warship decorated with distinctive "dazzle" camouflage.

🔟 ⭐ Isle of Skye

The product of violent geographical upheavals, the "Misty Isle" is justly famed for its towering, ragged mountains and wild coastline. Add to these a colourful patchwork of crofts (farms), waterfalls, an exceptional whisky distillery, a castle linked to the fairy-tale world and the historical romance of Bonnie Prince Charlie, and you find on Skye all the ingredients that best symbolize the Scottish Highlands.

Quiraing and the Old Man of Storr ④

A fantastic region of cliffs and pinnacles, one rocky outcrop (right) gaining the name the Old Man of Storr.

⑤ The Cuillins

This awesome range rises straight out of the sea to almost 1,000 m (3,300 ft). The Black Cuillins are a challenge even to seasoned climbers, but the Red Cuillins are an easier prospect for walkers.

① Loch Coruisk

The boat from Elgol passes seal colonies to reach this lovely loch (above), trapped in a bowl beneath the Cuillins – a prized view awaits.

⑥ Armadale Castle Gardens and Museum of the Isles

Beautiful coastal gardens surrounding the ruined castle of Clan MacDonald, with an historical archive.

② Aros Centre, Portree

An exceptional visitor and arts centre, created by locals with a passion for their culture. The place to learn about Skye's history and places to visit.

⑦ Dunvegan Castle

Dunvegan (left) was home to the chiefs of Clan MacLeod for 1,000 years. Find the Fairy Flag, which, it is said, can rally the "little people" to protect the clan.

Portree ③

Portree is Skye's mini capital, with some excellent shops and a delightful harbour lined by colourful buildings (right). Sailing races and Highland Games are big events in summer.

Previous pages Quiraing, Isle of Skye

**Map of
Isle of Skye**

FLORA MACDONALD

"Bonnie Prince Charlie" was pursued relentlessly by government troops following his defeat at Culloden. He escaped to Skye disguised as maidservant to the courageous Flora MacDonald. She was imprisoned for this act. On her release she emigrated to America, but later returned to Skye, where she died in 1790, one of the prince's bedsheets is her burial shroud.

⑩ Skye Museum of Island Life

Delightfully evocative, this reconstruction of thatched cottages **(below)**, or "blackhouses" (blackened by fire smoke), turns the years back a century or more.

⑧ Talisker Distillery

The so-called "lava of the Cuillins" is produced at Skye's only whisky distillery, where visitors are welcomed onto a friendly tour.

⑨ Island of Raasay

Its beauty often overlooked, Raasay offers land-based activities and watersports at its Outdoor Centre, or you can climb Dun Caan, the highest point on the island, for stunning views.

NEED TO KNOW

MAP D2

Aros Centre: (01478) 613 750; www.aros.co.uk

Armadale Castle: (01471) 844 305; open Apr–Oct: daily; adm £8.75

Dunvegan Castle: (01470) 521 206; open Apr–mid-Oct: daily; adm £14

Talisker Distillery, Carbost: (01478) 614 308; open Mar–Oct: 9:30am–5pm Mon–Sat (from 11am Sun); Nov–Mar: 10am–4:30pm daily; tours £10

Skye Museum of Island Life: (01470) 552206; open Easter–Oct: 9:30 am–5pm Mon–Sat; adm adults £3, children 50p; www.skyemuseum.co.uk

Misty Isle Boat Trips, Elgol: (01471) 866288

■ The Aros Centre has evenings of Gaelic culture with great local talent.

■ The Sligachan Hotel *(IV47 8SW; (01478) 650 204; www.sligachan.co. uk)*, 5 km (3 miles) west of Sconser, offers great bar meals and stunning views.

TOP 10 ⭐ Loch Ness and the Great Glen

A geological rift once split the land from coast to coast, dividing Scotland in two. Glaciers deepened the trench and the result today is a long glen of steep-sided, wooded mountains and dark, mysterious lochs. Castles and forts abound, bearing witness to the Great Glen's strategic importance and enhancing its dramatic grandeur with intrigue and nostalgia. And the legendary Loch Ness Monster, elusive but irrepressible, still attracts scientific interest.

1 Caledonian Canal

The canal **(below)** is an outstanding feat of engineering by Thomas Telford, connecting lochs Ness, Oich, Lochy and Linnhe. Watch boats glide past at Fort Augustus.

2 Loch Lochy

A path on this loch's **(below)** northern shore is now part of the Great Glen Walk and cycleway. Look out for the wonderful Cia Aig waterfall on the road to Loch Arkaig.

3 Fort William

Close to Glencoe and at the foot of Britain's highest mountain, Ben Nevis (1,345 m / 4,411 ft), this seaside town provides an ideal base for walkers. Almost every direction offers enticing terrain. The less active can scale Aonach Mor on the Nevis Range ski gondola or take the Jacobite Steam Train to Mallaig.

4 Great Glen Water Park

A sensitively landscaped centre among trees on Loch Oich, the smallest and most secluded in the glen. You can go canoeing, kayaking, canyoning, rock climbing or shoot the rapids on a raft.

5 Glen Affric

A lovely forest road leads to this renowned beauty spot. From here, a two-day hike can take you to the west coast.

TALES OF NESSIE

First recorded by St Aiden in the 7th century, "Nessie" pops up time and again. Despite many hoaxes and faked photographs, there's still a body of sonar and photographic evidence to support the existence of large creatures here, and scientific opinion remains open. To decide for yourself, visit one of the Loch Ness Monster information centres in Drumnadrochit, which present the evidence.

6 Inverness

The "Capital of the Highlands", Inverness is a bustling shopping centre set below a pink Victorian castle. The battlefield of Culloden *(see p38)* is nearby and the visitor centre there revives this sad and poignant event.

7 Urquhart Castle

Magnificently situated on the edge of Loch Ness, these ruins **(below)** were formerly one of Scotland's largest castles. A fine tower house still stands, and the views from the top are well worth the climb. The visitor centre is state-of-the-art and displays an array of medieval artifacts.

Map of Loch Ness and the Great Glen

NEED TO KNOW

MAP E3–D4

Jacobite Steam Train: (0844) 850 4685; open mid-May–Oct: Mon–Fri (mid-Jun–mid-Sep: daily)

Urquhart Castle: (01456) 450 551; open daily; adm adults £12, concessions £9.60, children £7.20

Fort George: (01667) 460 232; open daily; adm adults £9, concessions £7.20, children £5.40

Loch Ness Centre and Exhibition, Drumnadrochit: (01456) 450 573; open daily; adm £7.95, children £4.95

Jacobite Cruises (Canal and Loch Ness): (01463) 233 999; open daily

■ **Admission to most sights is free for Historic Scotland Members** *(check www.members.historic-scotland.gov.uk).*

■ **The Lock Inn** *(see p119)* has decent food.

8 Fort George

Built in the aftermath of Culloden on a sandy promontory in the Moray Firth, Fort George **(below)** is the mightiest artillery fortification in Britain. It is still in use as a barracks today, yet remarkably has only ever undergone minor modifications.

9 Loch Ness

Almost 230 m (750 ft) deep and 37 km (23 miles) long, Loch Ness is Scotland's largest waterbody. Flanked by mountains, castle and abbey ruins, and charming villages, Loch Ness is worthy of its fame. Jacobite lake cruises start from the north road along its bank. Other cruises leave from Inverness.

10 Fort Augustus

Fort Augustus is a delightful village situated on Loch Ness. Take a fading-sunlit, romantic evening walk in the grounds of the former abbey-school built in grand style in 1878.

🔟 ⭐ Glencoe

Nowhere else is the traveller confronted so abruptly by the arresting impact of Scotland's mountains. The road twists below the towering bulk of these characterful peaks, sometimes dark and louring, sometimes light and enticing. This ancient and celebrated pass is also imbued with history: cattle rustling, clan feuds and – most notoriously – the "Massacre of Glencoe" in 1692. In summer the area is a favourite haunt of walkers and climbers; in winter it is one of the leading ski resorts in the country.

① Glencoe Visitor Centre

This centre possesses a superb exhibition and audiovisual presentation – allow an hour to take it all in. A satellite weather report for the area is regularly updated; useful for walkers.

THE MASSACRE OF GLENCOE

Having signed an oath of submission to William III in 1692, albeit five days late, the MacDonald clan generously entertained and billeted 130 government soldiers in their homes for 10 days. The soldiers then slaughtered their hosts, leaving 38 dead. As much as the brutality of the massacre, it was the utter breach of trust that shocked the nation.

② Signal Rock, Glencoe Memorial and Forest Walk

A series of forest trails leads to the Signal Rock lookout **(left)**, where the MacDonalds *(see p43)* would light fires to send messages to clan members.

③ Invercoe Loch Walk and Pap of Glencoe

A particularly beautiful loch **(above)**, especially in May, when its rhododendrons are in full bloom. Behind looms the distinctive Pap of Glencoe peak, affording panoramic views.

④ Views of the Three Sisters

By a bend in the main road and next to a roaring waterfall, visitors will find a rocky knoll known as "The Study", which is a fine viewpoint for this trio of similarly profiled sibling mountains **(below)**.

Map of Glencoe

❻ ❷ ❽   ❼

North Ballachulish
● Kinlochleven
Glencoe ●
❶
Loch Linnhe   A82   ❾
A828   ❹
❺
Glasdrum ●
Gualachulain ●
❸   ❿

❿ Glencoe Ski Centre

Among the most popular of Scotland's five ski resorts **(below)**. All the year is available for hire in winter, and the terrain is ideal for snow thrills.

❼ Rannoch Moor

A beautiful but boggy wilderness, best seen from a window on the Fort William to Tyndrum train.

❽ Ice Factor

This exciting activity centre offers a wide range of indoor aerial adventures as well as outdoor courses. Their 12-m- (39-ft-) tall ice climbing wall is made of ice and snow, which weighs up to 500 tonnes. They feature a rock climbing wall too. Activities here are overlooked by professional instructors.

❺ Castle Stalker

A dreamlike castle **(below)**, alas not open to visitors but still magical to see, rising from an island that seems barely big enough to contain it.

❻ Loch Leven

The charming drive round this loch is punctuated by modest villages. Discover Glencoe's diverting museum and Kinlochleven's visitor centre that tells the story of 80 years of aluminium production here.

❾ Devil's Staircase

A tortuous section of the West Highland Way walk *(see p52)*, offering views to Rannoch Moor and Black Mount. The footpath continues to Kinlochleven for an even greater challenge.

NEED TO KNOW

MAP E3

Glencoe Visitor Centre: (01855) 811 307; open late Mar–late Oct: 9am–6pm daily; Oct–late Feb: 10am–4pm daily; adm £4 (free for National Trust for Scotland (NTS) members); www.nts.org.uk

Glencoe Folk Museum: (01855) 811 664; open Apr–Oct: Mon–Sat; adm £3; www.glencoe museum.com

Ice Factor: (01855) 831 100; open 9am–6pm daily; adm 1 hr sample session adult £30, junior £25 (12 yrs or above), 2.5 hr instructed ice climb £48; online booking available: www.ice-factor.co.uk

Glencoe Ski Centre: (01855) 851 226; Ski day pass: £32 (Jan–Apr), chairlift: £12 (Jul & Aug); www. glencoemountain.co.uk

■ Drive the scenic road that runs parallel to the A82 from Glencoe to the Clachaig Inn.

■ The craft shop in Glencoe has a good menu including delicious desserts.

TOP10 ⭐ Culzean Castle

Formerly a rather dull fortified tower house, Culzean (pronounced "Cullane") was transformed by the architect Robert Adam into a mansion of sumptuous proportions and elegance. The work began in 1777 and lasted almost 20 years, the Kennedy family sparing little expense in the decoration and craftsmanship of their clifftop home. Culzean – a masterpiece in a land full of magnificent castles – was gifted to the nation and fully restored in the 1970s. Its grounds became Scotland's first public country park in 1969.

4 Oval Staircase

Nothing short of perfection. Ionic and Corinthian capitals swirl above a Georgian-patterned carpet, lit up by an arched skylight **(left)**.

5 Home Farm Visitor Centre

No ordinary farm, but more of a fortified village within the country park; now it is a shop and restaurant.

Country Park 1

Known to be the most magnificent park in Britain **(right)**, this coastal swath of woodland, ponds, gardens, beaches and clifftop walks retains the Country Park's original character.

2 Lord Cassilis' Rooms

The restored late 18th-century decor includes vivacious Chinese-style wallpaper and a late Chippendale four-poster bed.

6 Round Drawing Room

The most beautiful room in the castle, with its circle of windows overlooking the sea.

3 Armoury

Over 1,000 weapons **(above)** cover the walls in concentric patterns. The fearsome arsenal includes the largest collection of used flintlock pistols in Europe.

ROBERT ADAM

Born in Kinross-shire in 1728, Robert Adam was educated at Edinburgh University. His subsequent tour of Italy determined his Neo-Classical style, and he went on to set up an architectural practice in London, becoming the foremost designer of his day. A true workaholic, his fanaticism for detail was legendary. Adam died in 1792, the year Culzean was completed.

7 Clifftop and Shoreline Trails

The views to the mountains of Arran are glorious from these trails. Two favourite destinations are Swan Pond and Happy Valley. Put on your walking boots and explore the glorious grounds.

Floorplan of Culzean Castle

Key to Floorplan
■ First floor
■ Ground floor

Culzean Castle and gardens

NEED TO KNOW

MAP G3 ■ Maybole ■ (01655) 884 455 ■ www.nts.org.uk

Open Apr–Oct: 10:30am–4:30pm daily; Nov–Mar: shops & restaurant only, 10am–5pm daily; Castle grounds: 9am–sunset daily

Adm (castle) adults £17; concessions £12.65; family £42.25; one-parent family £33.25; free for NTS members

■ It's all too easy to overlook half of the Walled Garden, and so miss the wonderful Victorian Vinery, where period species of dessert grapes are grown under glass.

9 Eisenhower Apartment

The apartment **(below)** on the top floor was a gift to the US president for his support in World War II. It is now a small hotel.

10 Long Drawing Room

Formerly the High Hall of the old tower house, this was the first room Adam transformed, and it was the first to be restored in the 1970s.

8 Camellia House

This impressive Gothic greenhouse **(below)** is one of more than 40 lesser architectural features found dotted around the grounds. It was designed in 1818 by James Donaldson, a pupil of Robert Adam.

TOP 10 ⭐ The Cairngorms

The highest mountain massif in the British Isles comprises a magnificent range of peaks, wild lochs and ancient forests, as well as bird sanctuaries, nature reserves and sports amenities. It is a region of exceptional scenery and habitats untouched by the road network. Activities take place on its fringe, but the heartland is open only to those who travel by foot or on skis. Its relative isolation makes it appealing for the wildlife that inhabits the region and for the people who thrive on the testing terrain.

1 Aviemore
Traditionally a dormitory town for skiers as well as the jumping-off point for touring the region at any time of the year, Aviemore consists of a concentration of hotels, guesthouses, bars, restaurants and après-ski (or, indeed, après-anything) entertainment.

2 Loch Morlich
Surrounded by the Caledonian pines of Rothiemurchus Forest, Loch Morlich **(above)** is a vast, tranquil lake at the base of the Cairngorms.

3 Loch an Eilean
Loch an Eilean is a hidden gem, 8 km (5 miles) from Aviemore. One of Scotland's best short walks is along this loch, nestling below the mountains. The trees are magnificent, and its crowning glory is an ivy-clad castle on an island.

5 Speyside Wildlife
A short drive from Aviemore, this hidden spot in the Caledonian pine forest is best for watching wildlife including badgers, pine martens **(left)** and more in the evening.

4 River Spey
Scotland's finest salmon river and birthplace of whisky, the Spey **(left)** is a river of dark pools and fast rapids. It winds through a variety of landscapes: moorland, forest, pasture and grain field.

Map of The Cairngorms

Grantown-on-Spey
Speybridge
Aviemore
Kingussie
Newtonmore
Spey

9 Malt Whisky Trail

The process of turning water into the "water of life" is a vital part of Scottish history and culture. Half of the nation's malt whisky distilleries are on Speyside **(above)**, and the signposted "whisky trail" leads the way to seven of them.

10 Cairngorm Reindeer Centre

Britain's only herd of wild reindeer **(right)** was introduced to Scotland in the 1960s. These charming animals, now numbering 150, roam free and are very friendly.

6 Loch Garten Osprey Centre

Ospreys began breeding here in 1954. More than 2 million visitors have now seen them from this hide. Vigilance has been necessary to foil egg-collectors.

7 Cairngorm Mountain Railway

This railway takes you almost to the top of Cairn Gorm mountain. The views are sublime, and at the Ptarmigan Restaurant & Bar you can enjoy the highest meal in the country.

8 Strathspey Steam Railway

The train **(below)** chuffs from Aviemore to Broomhill through a lovely landscape. It stops at Boat of Garten, famed for its Osprey Centre and a golf course.

NEED TO KNOW
MAP D4–5

Speyside Wildlife: (01479) 812 498; open Easter–Oct nightly; adm adult £25, children 8–14 yrs £10 (not suitable for under 14s); www.speysidewildlife.co.uk

Loch Garten Osprey Centre: (01479) 831 476; open Apr–Aug daily; adm adults £5

Cairngorm Mountain Railway: (01479) 861 261; closed for renovation; adm £13.50; www.cairngormmountain.org

Strathspey Steam Railway: (01479) 810 725; open Mar–Oct; return £15.75; www.strathspeyrailway.co.uk

Malt Whisky Trail: www.maltwhisky trail.com

Cairngorm Reindeer Centre: (01479) 861 228; guided hill visits 11am daily (May–Sep: 2:30pm); adm £3.50; tours £15; www.cairngormreindeer.co.uk

Spirit of Speyside Whisky Festival: open late Apr–early May; free to RSPB members; www.spiritofspeyside.com

The Top 10
of Everything

**The Forth Rail Bridge, spanning the
Firth of Forth near Edinburgh**

TOP10 Moments in History

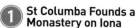
St Columba, the Irish missionary

1 St Columba Founds a Monastery on Iona

In 563 this fiery Irish missionary went into self-imposed exile on Iona (known as the "home of Christianity" in Europe), and here he founded a monastery. Columban monks travelled widely, consolidating the Christian faith and thus unifying Scotland's tribes into one nation.

2 Battle of Bannockburn

Facing an English onslaught in 1314, the Scots – led by Robert the Bruce – achieved a dazzling victory. By defeating the English, the Scots won back their nation and their pride. Their right to independence was ratified by papal bull in 1329, though the war with England continued for another 300 years.

Robert the Bruce

3 Battle of Flodden

To assist France, James IV invaded England in 1513 and met the enemy just over the border at Flodden. In the massacre that followed, some 10,000 Scots died,

James included, and, as his heir was still an infant, a power struggle and an era of instability ensued.

4 John Knox Leads the Reformation

Scotland was a Catholic country when Mary Queen of Scots ascended the throne. But in 1559, a revolutionary preacher called John Knox denounced Catholicism and heralded the Reformation. Protestantism was introduced to Scotland, and for the next 150 years religious intolerance was rife.

5 Union with England

When Elizabeth I died without an heir, James VI of Scotland succeeded her. He became James I of England in 1603, thus uniting the crowns. After Scotland was bankrupted by the disastrous Darien expedition, which failed to establish a colony in Panama, union with England became an economic necessity. The 1707 Act of Union united the Scottish and English parliaments, effectively dissolving Scottish Parliament.

6 Battle of Culloden

In 1745, James VII's grandson "Bonnie Prince Charlie" secretly sailed from France to Scotland to reclaim the British throne. He amassed an army which fought its way to a panic-stricken London. Short of their goal, the "Jacobites" returned north. The Hanoverian army, aided by royalist Scots, slaughtered the rebels at Culloden, the last battle fought on British soil.

7 Industrial Revolution

James Watt's transformation of the steam engine heralded the advent of the Industrial Revolution, which had a profound effect on

Glasgow in particular. The demand for steam forced every coalmine into maximum output, and the production of cotton, linen, steel and machinery boomed. Glasgow became known as "the workshop of the Empire".

Joseph Black visiting James Watt

8 World Wars and Emigration

Of the two world wars, it was the 1914–18 war that claimed the most lives: 74,000 Scottish soldiers and almost as many civilians. In addition to this, between 1901 and 1961, 1.4 million Scots emigrated to seek better lives elsewhere.

9 Return of a Scottish Parliament

In a 1997 referendum, the Scots emphatically voted to re-establish a Scottish Parliament. This opened in 1999, returning the political forum to the heart of Scotland after an absence of 292 years.

10 SNP Gains

Scotland voted against independence in 2014, but the Scottish National Party (SNP) gained 56 out of the 59 seats in Scotland in the 2015 UK election, though lost most of them in 2017. Scotland voted against Brexit, reviving desires for independence.

Nicola Sturgeon, leader of the SNP

TOP 10 WRITERS

Irvine Welsh, author of *Trainspotting*

1 John Barbour (c. 1316–96)
The "father of Scottish poetry", who wrote the epic poem, *The Brus*, in 1370.

2 Robert Burns (1759–96)
The famously nationalistic poet achieved a worldwide acclaim that titled him "the bard of humanity".

3 Sir Walter Scott (1771–1832)
The first best selling author, whose novels and poems launched a romantic tradition.

4 Robert Louis Stevenson (1850–94)
Best remembered for *Treasure Island*, this revered Edinburgh author travelled widely and died in Samoa.

5 Sir Arthur Conan Doyle (1859–1930)
Mastermind behind the Sherlock Holmes novels. He was born in Edinburgh and trained as a doctor.

6 J M Barrie (1860–1937)
Born in Kirriemuir, this novelist and dramatist established his reputation with the ever-popular *Peter Pan*.

7 Hugh MacDiarmid (1892–1978)
A Drunk Man Looks at the Thistle is considered the finest poem by the "pioneer of the Scottish Renaissance".

8 Iain Banks (1954–2013)
Hugely popular author of *The Crow Road*, and other psychological thrillers and science fiction.

9 Ian Rankin (1960–)
The creator of the hugely successful Inspector Rebus crime series was born in Fife, and now lives in Edinburgh.

10 Irvine Welsh (1961–)
Best-selling cult author of street culture in Scotland. Made his mark in 1993 with *Trainspotting*.

🔟 Castles

1 Edinburgh Castle

The greatest castle *(see pp12–13)* in a land that's full of them, not only prized for its crowning position in the capital's heart, but also for its important history and the national treasures it holds.

2 Culzean Castle

Architect Robert Adam's masterful design and exquisite taste reached their apotheosis in this castle *(see pp32–3)*, which ranks as one of Britain's finest mansions. Set in a park that does it ample justice, it commands a dramatic coastal position, looking seaward from the top of an Ayrshire cliff.

3 Caerlaverock Castle

A triangular ruin with immense towers, Caerlaverock *(see p88)* still sits within a filled moat. Its history spans a siege by King Edward I in 1300 and a luxurious upgrading shortly before its fall in 1640. Its yellow sandstone walls glow beautifully pink and orange in the afternoon light.

4 Stirling Castle

Dramatically perched on crags overlooking the plains where some of Scotland's most decisive battles took place, this castle *(see p103)* was one of the nation's greatest strongholds and a key player in her history. The gatehouse, Great Hall and the Renaissance Royal Palace are outstanding.

Check out the castle's programme of special events, from tapestry weaving to sword fights.

5 Glamis Castle

This 17th-century fairy-tale castle *(see p93)* is known for its literary associations: Duncan's Hall provided the setting for the king's murder in Shakespeare's *Macbeth*. It also has a famous secret chamber and was the childhood home of the late Queen Mother. Rooms represent different periods of history and contain fine collections of armour, furnishings and tapestries. The gardens were laid out by 18th-century landscape gardener "Capability" Brown. Besides an Italian garden there are other green spaces, including a walled garden that features fountains, fruits and vegetables. There are nature trails as well.

Glamis Castle

Eilean Donan Castle, on an island in Loch Duich

6 Balmoral

Queen Victoria purchased the Balmoral Estate in 1852 and transformed the existing castle into this imposing mansion set in spectacular grounds. Balmoral *(see p110)* is still the private holiday home of the British royal family, and provides an insight into contemporary stately living.

7 Dunnottar Castle

A glorious ruin *(see p109)* on a clifftop in Aberdeenshire with the sea crashing below, this is one of Scotland's most evocative sights. In the 17th century, the Scottish crown jewels were hidden here, away from Oliver Cromwell's marauding forces. The most scenic way to arrive at the castle is by the coastal footpath from Stonehaven.

8 Cawdor Castle

Whether or not the real Macbeth lived here in the 11th century, Cawdor *(see p111)* is the sort of make-believe castle that has come to life to satisfy all your Shakespearean expectations. The castle is utterly magical, with its original keep (1454), a drawbridge, ancient yew tree and enough weapons to start an uprising. The garden and estate are equally enchanting and there's even a maze to get lost in.

9 Eilean Donan Castle

One of Scotland's most photographed castles *(see p118)* because of its incredible setting – huddled on an island off the shores of Loch Duich and connected to the mainland by footbridge. This 13th-century stronghold of the Clan Macrae was left to ruin until its restoration in the 1930s.

10 Blair Castle

Seat of the Duke of Atholl, the only man in Britain still allowed a private army, this stately white castle *(see p91)* is an arresting sight off the A9, the main road north. The oldest part dates from 1269, but after damage during the Jacobite campaigns Blair Castle was completely restyled and all the turrets added.

Drawing room at Blair Castle

TOP 10 Highland Traditions

Highland dancers in traditional kilts

1 Scottish Dancing

Vital features of any Highland Games are the kilted dancers competing on stage. Among the most common Highland dances are Sword Dances – performed over crossed blades – and the Highland Fling. Look out for demonstrations of the ancient tradition of step dancing. While Highland dancing is performed by solo dancers, Scottish country dancing is a social dance.

2 Kilts and Tartans

The oldest tartan dates back to AD 245. It is unknown why Highlanders adopted this mode of dress, or when clans adopted a family "pattern" or tartan. The 1746 Dress Act banned Highland Dress in a purge on Highland culture. Today, tartans are flourishing, with over 2,000 registered designs.

3 Common Ridings

Known as the Riding of the Marches, this ritual dates back to the Middle Ages, when young men from the Border towns (such as Hawick) would ride out to check the boundaries of the town's common land. Each town has its own ceremony: the oldest is the Selkirk Gathering. Being one of the oldest equestrian events in the world, the Ridings take place early summer and may last several days.

4 Gaelic Language

The language of the Gael can be seen on road signs and heard in shops in the Highlands and Islands. There are estimated to be 60,000 Gaelic-speakers in the country, but even here it's a second language. Despite the rise in Gaelic education and success of Gaelic musicians, the country's youth appear less dedicated to the language causing a decline in its use.

5 Bagpipes

No sound is more evocative of Scotland than that of bagpipes. The great Highland pipes, dating back to at least the 14th century, are played by pipe and drum bands, and by individuals playing for competitions or dances. Over the last three decades bagpipes have emerged onto the stage of world music.

6 Curling

This sport (similar to bowls on ice) is one in which the Scots excel at in the Winter Olympics. Heavy circular granite stones, with a flat base and a handle on top, are used. The curler slides the stone down the rink towards a bull's-eye, and teammates, polish the path ahead of the stone if more momentum is needed.

Bagpipes

7 Shinty

This sport makes football look dull. Similar to anarchic hockey, this fast-moving game is entertaining. It takes place during winter and spring in the Highlands, culminating in the Camanachd Cup Final, the nearest thing to a re-enactment of Culloden.

8 Sabbatarianism

Sunday is still strictly observed as a day of rest in the Western Isles, and most local people attend church (with unique Gaelic psalm singing). Museums, attractions and public parks close, and some B&Bs do not take visitors. A limited ferry service exists, but plan your trip ahead of time.

9 Ceilidhs

Ceilidh ("cay-lee") is Gaelic for "a visit among friends", but has taken on the meaning of "a party". Sometimes it is a hall with a band where everyone dances. At other times it is a communal performance where people sing, dance or play an instrument in turns. They are great fun and even ceilidhs held in the smallest of village halls host world-class local or touring performers.

10 Highland Games

This summer spectacle is packed with bagpipes, dancers and athletes, and forms an essential part of any visit. Most popular are the kilted strongmen in the "heavy events", which include hurling monstrous hammers as well as tossing a tree trunk.

The caber toss, Highland Games

TOP 10 CLANS AND TARTANS

Monument to the MacDonalds clan

1 The MacDonalds
Most powerful of all the clans, they hold the title 'Lords of the Isles'.

2 The Campbells
Members of this feared clan murdered their MacDonald hosts at Culloden.

3 The MacLeods
This clan has Norse heritage. Their chief still lives at Dunvegan Castle, on the Isle of Skye.

4 The Stewarts
With a bright red tartan, they were the descendants of Scotland's royal dynasty.

5 The Gordons
Famed for their soldiering skills, the motto of their clanv was 'by courage, not by craft'.

6 The Sinclairs
The origins of this clan are Norman and the main branch of the family is headed by the Earl of Caithness.

7 The MacKays
The name, meaning 'son of fire', comes from Gaelic. They supported the government during the Jacobite rising of 1745.

8 The Mackenzies
Associated with the north west highlands, their stronghold once was the much photographed Eilean Donan castle.

9 The MacNeils
This clan, associated with Barra, were said to be notorious pirates. They launched raids from vessels similar to Viking longboats.

10 The MacIntyres
The name in Gaelic is Mac an t-Saoir, which means 'son of the carpenter'. They were originally associated with Skye and later Loch Etive in Argyll.

🔟 Lochs

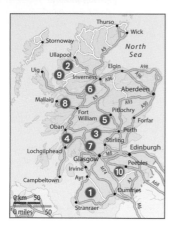

1 Loch Trool
MAP H4

An enchanting loch within a forest, in a very much overlooked corner of Scotland, characterized by its stunning wilderness. The loch is bordered by walks, which form part of the long-distance Southern Upland Way *(see p52)*. At the eastern end there's a memorial to King Robert the Bruce, King of Scots from 1306 until his death in 1329.

2 Loch Maree
MAP C3

You'll pass this loch if you visit Inverewe Gardens *(see p49)*. Wonderfully situated among imposing mountains, Loch Maree is a revered fishing location next to a nature reserve. Red deer have been known to swim out to the group of wooded islands in the centre and make temporary homes there.

Picturesque Loch Maree

3 Loch Katrine
MAP F4

Famous as the inspiration for Sir Walter Scott's poem *Lady of the Lake*, this loch is the pearl of the area known as the Trossachs. Now incorporated into the National Park with Loch Lomond *(see p103)*, it is sheer tranquillity compared with the other's bustle. A boat tour here is highly recommended – the SS *Sir Walter Scott* (naturally) has been doing the job for over a century.

4 Loch Awe
MAP F3

A long sliver of a loch, twisting through forested hills. The magnificent ruins of the 13th-century Kilchurn Castle *(see p106)* stand at one end and testify to the stormy past of clan Campbell *(see p43)*. Take the southern road for the best scenery, and don't be in a hurry. Close by is the defunct but preserved Bonawe Iron Foundry.

Ruins of Kilchurn Castle at Loch Awe

5 Loch Tummel
MAP E4

This small loch, with its shimmering brilliance, was a favourite of Queen Victoria, and you can stand at her

Lush forest around Loch Tummel

preferred spot on the north side at Queen's View. The vista to the distant peak of Schiehallion *(see p47)* is splendid, complemented in autumn by sweeps of colourful forest. Take the southern road to find the best picnic spots by the loch, and don't miss the river gorge walks at nearby Killiecrankie *(see p94)*.

6 Loch Ness
MAP D4

Probably Scotland's most charismatic loch *(see pp28–9)*, this deep body of water is a major draw for its scenic splendour of the Great Glen, Urquhart Castle and the as-yet-unexplained sightings of monster Nessie.

7 Loch Lomond

The largest surface of fresh water in Scotland, Loch Lomond's *(see p103)* beauty is celebrated in literature, song and legend. Forming part of Scotland's first National Park, in conjunction with the Trossachs, the loch is revered for its islands, lofty hills and shoreside leisure facilities.

8 Loch Morar

The rival to Loch Ness, Loch Morar *(see p120)* is Scotland's deepest loch at over 300 m (1,000 ft), and has long had its own legend of a monster – Morag (apparently identical to Nessie). Morar is easy to get to but little visited because its shores are largely inaccessible to cars, which makes it all the more delightful for walking *(see p58)*. Nearby are spectacular beaches – the White Sands of Morar.

9 Loch Torridon
MAP D3

A magnificent sea loch that is reminiscent of a Norwegian fjord. The wall of red sandstone mountains to its north attracts hill walkers, and from the summits you can see all the way from Cape Wrath *(see p129)* to Ardnamurchan *(see p118)*. A lovely one-way walk takes you from Diabeg to Inveralligin, with a series of refreshing lochans (small lochs) in which to swim if the weather's hot.

10 Loch Skeen
MAP G5

The hidden treasure at the end of an utterly magical walk, Loch Skeen is a tiny loch high up in moorland hills. The walk to it climbs steeply alongside the spectacular Grey Mare's Tail waterfall (note that it's dangerous to leave the path en route). The visitor centre, situated near the falls, has a CCTV on a peregrine falcon nest.

TOP 10 Munros

1 Ben Nevis

Britain's highest mountain (see p117) at 1,345 m (4,411 ft). A long, winding path takes you up to the top. The summit is seldom clear of cloud, but if you strike it lucky you'll enjoy unsurpassed views. In poor visibility take great care on the summit ridge as it's easy to lose the path, which borders a precipice.

Climbing Ben Nevis

2 Ben Cruachan
MAP E3

A grouping of seven peaks overlooking lochs Awe (see p44) and Etive. The highest is 1,126 m (3,694 ft) and as this summit is considerably taller than any other mountain in the area, Ben Cruachan enjoys some of the most extensive views in the country. The name "Cruachan" comes from the war cry of the Campbell clan (see p43).

3 Ben Macdui
MAP D5

Britain's second-highest mountain, at 1,309 m (4,295 ft), is best climbed from the Cairngorm ski car park. Reached by a high-altitude plateau covered in Arctic flora, it overlooks the magnificent Lairig Ghru, a deep rift dividing the Cairngorm range.

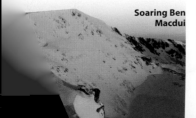

Soaring Ben Macdui

DEFINITION OF A MUNRO

Any Scottish summit over 3,000 ft (approx. 900 m) is called a "Munro" after Sir Hugh Munro, who published a list of them in 1891. There are 282 Munros, and "Munro-bagging" is a popular pastime. Most can be walked safely without climbing skills, but it is vital to plan well and be properly equipped and competent in map-reading. Conditions can deteriorate rapidly at any time of year.

4 Ben Vorlich
MAP F4

A great one to start with as there's nothing complicated about this hill, which overlooks Loch Earn, always bustling with boat activity. Take the southern road and start from Ardvorlich. At the top, at 985 m (3,232 ft), the views to the Breadalbane mountains are glorious. After drinking it in and taking some panoramic snaps, it doesn't take long to get down for tea in St Fillans.

5 Ben Lomond
MAP F4

Rising proudly from the wooded banks of its namesake loch, Ben Lomond's tall mass dominates the panorama. One of the smallest Munros at 973 m (3,192 ft), it has a well-used track, which is steep in places. There are tremendous views over the Loch Lomond and Trossachs National Park (see p103). It is best to start at Rowardennan, where there's a hotel and hostel.

6 Ben Hope
MAP B4

The most northerly Munro, with its neighbour, Foinaven. Rising starkly from the woods and moorland around Loch Hope, 927-m (3,040-ft) Ben Hope has clear views to the Orkneys. The only difficulty in bagging this peak is the scree and rocky terrain, but this is a prestigious mountain to have underfoot.

The Five Sisters, reflected in the waters of Loch Duich

7 The Five Sisters
MAP D3

A superb range of mountains with five prominent peaks towering above Glen Shiel in the West Highlands. Start at the highest part of the main road (A87) to save yourself an hour's climbing. Once you're on the summit ridge it's a long series of undulations, but you feel on top of the world and can see the Cuillins on Skye *(see pp26–7)*.

8 Buchaille Etive Mor
MAP E3

The 1,021-m- (3,350-ft-) tall "Great Shepherd of Etive" stands as guardian to the eastern entrance to Glencoe *(see pp30–31)*. As an introduction to a place of legendary beauty, this wild mountain could not be improved. Approached from the southwest it can be climbed easily, but its magnificent crags demand respect.

9 Schiehallion
MAP E4

A much-loved mountain between lochs Tay and Rannoch, Schiehallion is most easily climbed from the pretty road connecting Aberfeldy with Tummel Bridge. An easy and rewarding Munro with which to launch your bagging campaign.

10 Liathach
MAP D3

You could pick any of the famous Torridon mountains *(see p116)* and guarantee not to be disappointed, but this is a particular beauty. A massive mound of red sandstone topped with white quartzite, Liathach has distinctive parallel bands of escarpments. At 1,055 m (3,461 ft), this is a relatively difficult and strenuous mountain to climb, but worth every bit of effort.

Atlantic Ocean
Thurso
Wick
Scourie 6
Stornoway
North Sea
Ullapool
Tain
Elgin A98
Uig 10
Shieldaig
Inverness A96
Sligachan 7
Aviemore 3 A93
Mallaig A87
Fort William 1
Pitlochry A90
Isle of Mull 8 9
Oban 2
Perth
Lochgilphead 4
5 Stirling
M9
0 km 50
Glasgow Edinburgh
0 miles 50

Liathach from Loch na Frianach

TOP 10 Gardens

Rock garden at the Royal Botanic Garden, Edinburgh

1 Royal Botanic Garden

Edinburgh's prize garden (see p76), founded in 1670 and moved to its current site in 1820, features huge trees, rock terraces and borders bursting with colour. The glasshouses are of particular interest, containing everything from hothouse palm trees and gigantic lilies to dwarf cactuses and orchids. Watch out for special events, such as music, theatre and exhibitions of contemporary art.

2 Dawyck Botanic Garden

MAP G5 ■ Stobo, nr Peebles ■ (01721) 760254 ■ Open Apr–Sep: 10am–6pm daily (Mar & Oct: to 5pm; Feb & Nov: to 4pm) ■ Adm

An outpost of Edinburgh's Royal Botanic Garden, where trees are the speciality. They began planting them here 300 years ago. With its enormous diversity and fine specimens, the garden is ideal for woodland walks. The visitor centre has a café, a shop and exhibitions.

3 Kailzie Gardens

MAP G5 ■ Kailzie, nr Peebles ■ (01721) 720007 ■ Open Apr–Oct: 10am–5pm daily; Nov–Mar: daylight hours daily ■ Adm ■ www.kailzie gardens.com

This formal walled garden is an outstanding example of what was once more common on family estates. Marvellous roses fill the air with fragrance, and there's a pond stocked with trout for fishing.

4 Logan Botanic Garden

MAP H3 ■ Port Logan, south of Stranraer ■ (01776) 860231 ■ Open mid-Mar–Oct: 10am–5pm daily (Nov: to 4pm; Feb: to 4pm Sun only) ■ Adm

The Logan boasts the largest number of exotic species growing outdoors in Scotland. The southern hemisphere is particularly well represented; the palm trees and gunnera have grown to almost jungle proportions. Apart from the climate, there's a South Pacific feel to the place. It's usually much quieter than other gardens.

5 Botanic Gardens, Glasgow

Positively bulging with greenery and colour, Glasgow's Botanic Gardens (see p99) are a favourite with locals and visitors alike. The magnificent gardens date from 1817, and are particularly noted for their glasshouses. Foremost among these is the curved iron framework of the restored Kibble Palace. An oasis of palm trees, ferns, orchids, begonias and many exotic species is found inside. Art exhibitions, theatre, festivals and plant shows also take place here.

6 Crarae Gardens

Created in 1912 by Lady Grace Campbell, this Himalayan-style woodland garden (see p104) has one of the country's most diverse collections of rhododendrons. Many of the seeds were gathered on private expeditions around the world and some species are now rare. In May the garden bursts into a mass of blooms. It is also home to the National Collection of southern beech trees. There is a waterfall, a gorge and several walking trails.

7 Arduaine Gardens

Overlooking the sea, this garden (see p104) was established in 1898. It is another famous rhododendron collection, but includes exotic blue Tibetan poppies, giant Himalayan lilies, lush magnolias, camellias, tree ferns, water lilies and Chatham Island forget-me-nots. Having fallen into disrepair, Arduaine was lovingly restored by two brothers. See wildlife such as red squirrels in the woods, or spot seals and porpoises at the sea shore.

Plants at The Hydroponicum

8 The Hydroponicum

A totally revolutionary place, the "garden of the future" (see p120) has no soil but uses a clever water irrigation system to carry nutrients to the plants. Take a tour of the growing houses where they cultivate everything from tropical flowers to bananas. You can buy your own growing kits and fresh seasonal produce.

9 Inverewe Gardens

A west coast phenomenon, these much-vaunted gardens (see p119) are worth travelling a long way to see. The gardens were nurtured into astonishing fertility in 1862 by Scottish aristocrat Osgood Mackenzie on his 8.5-sq-km (3-sq-mile) estate, and they became his life's work. Exotic plants, shrubs and trees from all over the world form one of the finest botanical collections in the country, all in a stunning location on Loch Ewe.

10 Pitmedden Garden

Originally laid out in a Classical French style in 1675 and destroyed by a fire in 1818, Pitmedden (see p109) was meticulously recreated in the 1950s. The effect is stunning. Within a vast walled area are four elaborate floral parterres, three of which have heraldic designs.

Rhododendrons, Arduaine Gardens

TOP 10 Walking Routes

Breathtaking sights from Conic Hill, West Highland Way

1 West Highland Way
MAP E3–F4 ▪ 154 km (96 miles) ▪ 7–10 days ▪ www.westhighlandway.org

The first long-distance route, and still the most popular. Connecting Fort William and Glasgow, it winds past the Nevis and Glencoe ranges, crosses Rannoch Moor and skirts around every other mountain it can find. Stunning scenery, but rather close to the main road in parts.

2 Southern Upland Way
MAP H3–F6 ▪ 344 km (214 miles) ▪ 15–20 days ▪ www.southernuplandway.gov.uk

The longest walking route in Scotland, and a wonderful mix of mountain, moor, forest, loch and pasture. It crosses the country from Portpatrick in the west to Cockburnspath in the east – the preferred direction if you want the wind at your back.

3 Great Glen Way
MAP D4–E3 ▪ 127 km (79 miles) ▪ 4–7 days ▪ www.greatglenway.com

This popular long-distance route probably packs in more dramatic scenery per mile than any other. The walk connects Fort William with Inverness. The southern half offers easier gradients along the banks of lochs Lochy and Oich. After Fort Augustus it climbs high above Loch Ness – if that doesn't take your breath, the views will.

4 Speyside Way
MAP D4–C5 ▪ 105 km (66 miles) ▪ 4–6 days ▪ www.speysideway.org

Bordering one of Scotland's most picturesque rivers, this path takes you from the Cairngorms to Moray's coast (with spurs to Dufftown and Tomintoul). It is a walk full of interest, with distilleries galore, bridges, stately homes and a rich abundance of wildlife.

5 Border Abbeys Way
MAP G5–6 ▪ 105 km (65 miles) ▪ 4–5 days ▪ www.borderabbeysway.com

Border Abbeys Way is a circular route that combines historical interest with the irresistible appeal of the gentle Borders landscape, with its rounded hills, rivers and forests. The track connects the four magnificent abbeys of Kelso, Melrose, Dryburgh and Jedburgh.

Previous pages Steam train crossing the Glenfinnan Viaduct on the West Highland Line

6 Cateran Trail

MAP E5 ■ 103 km (64 miles)
■ 5 days ■ www.pkct.org/cateran-trail

The Caterans, brigands and rustlers roamed this area in the Middle Ages. Starting in Blairgowrie's soft-fruit hills, this circular route wends to the wild mountains of Glenshee, returning via beautiful Glenisla, offering some of the best of Perthshire. This is a quieter trail than most.

7 Fife Coastal Path

MAP F5 ■ 188 km (117 miles)
■ 6–9 days ■ www.fifecoastal path.co.uk

This walk connects the famous Forth and Tay bridges. It runs from North Queensferry, near Deep Sea World, to the small fishing villages of the East Neuk such as Elie and Anstruther, which huddle beside rugged cliffs. The route then heads north, through the historic town and golfing capital of St Andrews.

Newark Castle, Fife Coastal Path

8 St Cuthbert's Way

MAP G5–6 ■ 100 km (62 miles)
■ 4 days ■ www.stcuthbertsway.info

This is the only cross-border route in Scotland. It starts in the abbey town of Melrose and ends on the amazing island of Lindisfarne (England). It is not too strenuous a walk and a lovely mix of pasture, woodland, moor and coastal scenery. Be sure to check the tides for the last mile.

9 Loch Lomond and Cowal Way

MAP F3 ■ 92 km (57 miles)
■ 7 days ■ www.lochlomondand cowalway.org

If you like things a little wilder, try this one. The route is fully way-marked, and passes through some of Scotland's most varied landscapes. marked, so take a good map. Start on the coast west of Glasgow at Portavadie and cross the hills of the Cowal peninsula to Inveruglas on the shores of Loch Lomond.

10 John Muir Way

MAP F4–6 ■ 215 km (134 miles) ■ 7–10 days
■ www.johnmuirway.org

This route runs coast to coast, from Helensburgh in the west to Dunbar in the east. Named for John Muir, father of America's National Parks, who was born in Dunbar; his birthplace is a museum.

John Muir Way

🔟 Journeys

The West Highland Line crossing the River Orchy at Loch Awe

1 West Highland Line

MAP D2–F4 ■ ScotRail: www.scotrail.co.uk ■ Jacobite Steam Train: www.westcoastrailways.co.uk

The West Highland Line runs from Glasgow to Mallaig. The journey takes around 5 hours and 30 minutes, and the train stops frequently, giving the chance to relax and enjoy the sights of Scotland's west coast. Look out for the Glenfinnan Viaduct, which featured in the *Harry Potter* films, as well as views of Ben Nevis and Loch Eilt. If you want to travel in style take the Jacobite Steam Train which runs in summer.

2 Take Flight

Loch Lomond Seaplanes: (01436) 675 030; www.lochlomond-seaplanes.com ■ Loganair: www.loganair.co.uk ■ Flybe: www.flybe.com

Seaplane, Loch Lomond

Soar over Loch Lomond or the Isle of Skye with Loch Lomond Seaplanes. The seaplane offers spectacular views of Scotland's lochs and mountains. Tours should be booked ahead. Another exhilarating flight is from Glasgow to Barra with Flybe or Loganair. The island's runway is on a beach and disappears under the waves when the tide comes in.

3 Borders Railway

MAP F5–G5 ■ www.bordersrailway.co.uk

Opened in 2015 and stretching 48 km (30 miles) between Edinburgh and Tweedbank, the Borders Railway is the longest railway line to be built in Britain for 100 years. Tweedbank station is a short walk from Abbotsford House, home of Sir Walter Scott.

4 The Road to the Isles

MAP D2–E3

The A830 from Fort William to Mallaig is known as the 'Road to the Isles'. This is Bonnie Prince Charlie country and is crammed with Jacobite history. Driving it gives you the freedom to stop and explore sights, such as Glenfinnan, where Charles Edward Stuart placed his standard in 1745 and rallied the clans in his attempt to regain the crown; and Loch nan Uamh, from where he fled to France after being defeated at Culloden.

5 Steam Back in Time
MAP F1 ▪ www.waverley
excursions.co.uk

A trip "doon the watter" on the PS *Waverley*, the world's last seagoing paddle steamer, is a classic Scottish journey that all ages can enjoy. Launched in 1946 and originally fuelled by coal, the ship was saved from the breaker's yard in the 1970s and is now owned by a charity. Take a summer day trip from Glasgow to destinations such as Dunoon, Rothesay and Arran. Special excursions run too.

6 Climb a Mountain
www.cairngormmountain.co.uk

From the gentler slopes of the Eildon Hills in the Borders, to the mighty peak of Ben Nevis, Scotland's hills and mountains are wild, beautiful, challenging and irresistible. If you are not an experienced walker you can enjoy the view by taking the funicular railway up Cairn Gorm mountain (*see p35*). There's a restaurant and viewing platform at the top.

7 Pedal a Trail
7 Stanes Centres:
www.7stanes.com

Whether you're a novice or an experienced biker, you're sure to find a trail to suit you in Scotland. There are demanding routes such as the Sligachan on Skye, a single-track circuit almost 45 km (28 miles) long. The 7 Stanes Centres, in Dumfries and Galloway and the Borders, offer trails to suit all abilities. They have centres at Dalbeattie, Glentrool, Ae, Kirroughtree, Mabie, Glentress and Innerleithen and Newcastleton.

Bike trail

8 Bridge the Forth
MAP F5

When it opened in 1890, the Forth Bridge was the world's longest single-span cantilevered bridge, and it's still an iconic structure. Appreciate this Victorian marvel by taking the train across it – travelling from Edinburgh or South Queensferry into Fife.

9 Ferry Crossing
Calmac: www.calmac.co.uk
▪ Skye Ferry: operates Easter–Oct: 10am–6pm (Jun–Aug: to 7pm); www.skyeferry.co.uk

A ferry-trip to a Scottish island is a wonderfully romantic experience. The main operators, Calmac, run services to islands – Arran, Skye and the Inner and Outer Hebrides. Ferries also run between Gourock and Dunoon and connect with trains from Glasgow Central. Scotland's last manually operated turntable ferry, the Skye Ferry, sails between Glenelg on the mainland and Kylerhea on Skye.

10 North Coast 500
MAP B5–D4 ▪ www.north
coast500.com

The North Coast 500 is an 800-km (500-mile) circuit. From Inverness, the route goes west to Applecross then up the coast and along the tip of Scotland to John O'Groats, from where it heads back down to Inverness.

TOP 10 Golf Courses

1 St Andrews

Every golfer dreams of playing here (see p92). There are seven courses, including the famous Old Course. Book months in advance or take your chance in the lottery for unreserved places held the day before. Fit in a visit to the Golf Museum too, home to 17,000 objects showing the history of golf from the Middle Ages to the present. The restaurant at the Old Course Hotel (see p95) is excellent.

Playing at the Old Course, St Andrews

2 Turnberry
MAP G3 ■ (01655) 331 000
■ www.turnberry.co.uk

Purchased by Donald Trump in 2014 and situated on the Ayrshire coast, the Ailsa Course has tested all the world's great players. A new 18-hole course, King Robert the Bruce, opened in 2017. For expert tuition and a review of your game, contact the Golf Academy, a multi-million-pound addition to the hotel.

3 Carnoustie Championship Course
MAP E5 ■ (01241) 802 270
■ www.carnoustiegolflinks.co.uk

A delightful course, the superb links and great character of which have earned it a world-class reputation. You'll need to present your handicap certificate to play here and reserve your tee time in advance, but there are two other good links if you don't get on the main one. Saturdays can be busy throughout the year.

4 Gullane
MAP F5 ■ (01620) 842 255
■ www.gullanegolfclub.co.uk

Almost every blade of grass in the East Lothian corner is dedicated to golf. Muirfield is the elite course but a private club. Gullane No. 1 is open to anyone (handicap certificate required), while Nos. 2 and 3 have no restrictions. If Gullane is crowded, drive a short way to North Berwick, Haddington or Aberlady, and seven more top courses.

5 Muirfield
MAP F5 ■ Gullane ■ (01620) 842 123 ■ www.muirfield.org.uk

This 18-hole championship course dates back to 1891, when it was first laid out by Tom Morris. Situated in lush East Lothian, by the pretty village of Gullane, it is home to the Honourable Company of Edinburgh Golfers. Visitors' days are Tuesday and Thursday. Availability of tee times can be checked in advance.

The grand Turnberry Hotel

Fairway bunkers on Gleneagles golf course

6 Gleneagles
MAP F4 ▪ (01764) 662 231
▪ www.gleneagles.com

Another legendary group of courses, in beautiful moorland attached to a luxurious hotel. There are three championship courses, including the PGA Centenary that was designed by Jack Nicklaus. There is also the PGA National Academy, a nine-hole course, which is ideal for beginners There is a delectable restaurant here (see p95).

7 Troon
MAP G4 ▪ Old Course & Portland: (01292) 311 555; www. royaltroon.co.uk ▪ Darley, Fullarton, Lochgreen, Kilmarnock: (01292) 616 255; www.golfsouthayrshire.com/ courses

Among the six courses here there's one for everyone, from Fullarton's fun course for beginners to the classics such as Darley and Portland. But the best is the Old Course, a vintage Open venue. You need to apply well in advance.

8 Old Prestwick
MAP G4 ▪ (01292) 477 404
▪ www.prestwickgc.co.uk

New courses come and steal the limelight but Old Prestwick glows as an enduring favourite. In 1860 it was the first venue to hold the British Open Championship. It remains a challenging course and one of Scotland's most venerated. Very busy, especially at weekends.

9 Royal Dornoch
MAP C4 ▪ (01862) 810 219
▪ www.royaldornoch.com

The championship course has 18 pristine holes. It was laid out by Tom Morris in 1877 and follows the natural contours of the dunes around Dornoch Bay. A wonderful setting and less pressurized than other quality links.

10 Nairn
MAP D4 ▪ Nairn: (01667) 453 208; www.nairngolfclub.co.uk ▪ Nairn Dunbar: (01667) 452 741; www.nairn dunbar.com

There are two championship courses here. The Nairn hosts major tournaments but also has a nine-hole course, the Cameron, for holiday golfers. Nairn Dunbar is the other top-notch course.

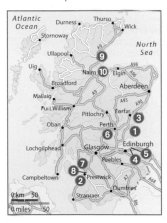

 Off the Beaten Track

Boats moored by the entrance to Morar River

1 Walk from Loch Morar to Tarbet

MAP E3 ■ 20 km (12 miles); approx 6 hours ■ Book the ferry in advance: (01687) 462 233

A combined walk and boat trip through sublime scenery. From Morar's silver sands, follow Britain's shortest river (half a mile) to the loch. Tarred at first, the way turns into an undulating track, which wends to its destination at the lovely bay of Tarbet. Arrive by 3:30pm to catch the ferry back to Mallaig.

2 Old Forge Music Venue

MAP D3 ■ Inverie
■ (01687) 462 267

The Old Forge offers legendary music sessions, open fires, superb, unpretentious food and free moorings if you arrive by boat. The sea almost laps at the door, and Knoydart's scenery is among the best. The Old Forge has been classed by the *Guinness World Records* as the most remote pub in mainland Britain.

3 Sunset from Craig Mountain Bothy

MAP C3 ■ Mountain Bothies Association: www.mountainbothies. org.uk

A simple, isolated cottage with five-star views over the sea to Skye and the Western Isles – sunsets are utterly breathtaking. Only accessible by foot, Craig is 5 km (3 miles) from

Little Diabeg or 9 km (5 miles) from Red Point – and a lovely walk it is, too. You'll need to bring all provisions and a sleeping bag, and bear in mind there's no phone on site.

4 Falls of Foyers

MAP D4

The more rain, the merrier for this one, so leave your visit until after a wet day. The upper falls are impressive; the lower falls even more so, plunging a spectacular 62 m (200 ft). The yellow-white torrent gushes into a black bowl, hollowed deep in the forest near Loch Ness, and the almighty roar of the rushing water is as awe-inspiring as the magnificent sight itself.

Falls of Foyers on the River Foyers

⑤ Elie Chain Walk
MAP F5

As exciting as it is short, this 2.5-km (1.5-mile) cliff walk involves steep carved steps and chains bolted into rock to allow high-tide access between the coves. The best route is to walk west along the cliffs from the small town of Elie, descend to sea level at the tip of the headland, and then return along the chain walk. The chains are inaccessible for 2 hours at high tide, and are unnecessary at low tide.

⑥ Knoydart
MAP D3 ■ www.knoydart-foundation.com

The most remote part of mainland Britain, this peninsula of rugged hills and glens lies in a time warp that's inaccessible by car. However, regular ferries from Mallaig provide access to the village of Inverie and outdoor activities including guided walks and mountain biking. Knoydart is a favourite destination for landscape photographers, which says much about its beauty.

Loch Hourn, Knoydart

⑦ Drive from Ullapool to Kylesku
MAP C3–B3

Scotland's most beautiful road. Drive it in spring when it's almost consumed by yellow-flowering whins, or in winter when surf erupts against the shore, or on a blue summer evening when Assynt's mountains assume the shape of absurd scribbles. But do drive it: take the A835 north from Ullapool, go west at Drumrunie, follow signs to Lochinver, then the B869 to Kylesku.

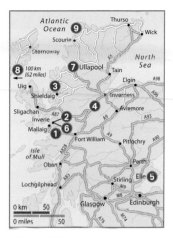

⑧ St Kilda
www.kilda.org.uk

Scotland's first World Heritage Site, this archipelago of monumental cliffs was, until 1930, inhabited by a highly individual community who lived off the islands' millions of seabirds. Such is St Kilda's isolation that it has its own subspecies of mouse, wren and sheep. Hard to get to, but if you can it'll touch your soul.

⑨ Sandwood Bay
MAP B3 ■ Nr Kinlochbervie

Perhaps it's the colourful strata patterning the rocks (Lewisian gneiss, among the world's oldest) or the quality of the sand. Perhaps it's the huge stack that stands sentinel at one end like some antediluvian shepherd. Or the Atlantic waves that charge in with billowing crests. Or is it the fact that so often you can have this expanse of beach to yourself?

⑩ Regional Feis
Feb–Oct ■ Feisean nan Gaidheal: (01478) 613 355 ■ www.feisean.org

A feis ("faysh") is a festival of Gaelic arts combined with workshops. Lasting several days, most take place in the Highlands and islands, always with terrific performances and blistering dances.

🔟 Children's Attractions

Go Ape treetop trail

1 Go Ape
www.goape.co.uk

Enjoy zip-wiring and treetop thrills in Glentress Forest, near Peebles; Crathes Castle *(see p112)*, near Aberdeen and Queen Elizabeth Forest Park, near Loch Lomond – the last includes a 400-m (1,300-ft) zip wire over a 27-m- (90-ft-) high waterfall.

2 Museum of Childhood
A feast of nostalgia, with toys from the 18th to 21st centuries, this place *(see p15)* is a real family attraction. It features everything – from teddy bears to Teletubbies, Meccano sets to snakes and ladders, comics to satchels and slates. Highlights include a wooden doll dating to around 1740, a tiny Steiff teddy bear which travelled out of Vienna in 1939 on the last Kindertransport train and a dolls house with electric lighting.

3 Our Dynamic Earth
Housed in a spiked tent, this electrifying exhibition *(see p76)* is a mix of education and entertainment. You travel through all sorts of environments, from volcanic eruptions to the Ice Ages. Stand on shaking floors, get caught in a tropical downpour, fly over prehistoric Scottish glaciers and come face-to-face with extinct dinosaurs. The exhibition also goes further, looking at our future and pondering the realities of climate change.

4 M&D's Scotland's Theme Park
MAP F4 ■ Motherwell ■ (01698) 333 777 ■ Open mid-Mar–mid-Oct: phone or check website for times ■ Adm ■ www.scotlandsthemepark.com

Huge fairground fun centre with everything that gravitational and centrifugal forces can do to you. Big wheel, free-fall machine, flying carpet, kamikaze whirligigs and the giant "500 tons of twisted fun" roller-coaster. For the younger children there are gentler water chutes and merry-go-rounds. There's also Amazonia, an indoor tropical rainforest.

5 Kelburn Country Centre
MAP F3 ■ Nr Largs ■ (01475) 568 685 ■ Adventure Park & Secret Forest: open Apr–Oct: 10am–6pm daily ■ Grounds: open all year ■ Adm ■ www.kelburnestate.com

The family estate of the Earls of Glasgow doubles as an adventure park. The surprise-packed Secret Forest gets the best vote, and kids will go berserk in the indoor play barn and adventure play areas. Various events, a 12th-century castle decorated with graffiti and well-organized pony treks.

Runaway Timber Train ride at Landmark Forest Adventure Park

6 Landmark Forest Adventure Park

MAP D4 ■ Carrbridge, nr Aviemore ■ (0800) 731 3446 ■ Open Apr–Oct: 10am–6pm daily (mid-July–mid-Aug: to 7pm; closing times vary, check website) ■ Adm ■ www.landmarkpark.co.uk

A play and adventure centre based around a tree theme. Join the fun in the Lost Labyrinth, climb 105 steps of the timber tower or ride the Runaway Timber Train. There's also a delightful climbing apparatus.

7 Glasgow Science Centre

MAP Y3 ■ 50 Pacific Quay, Glasgow ■ (0141) 420 5000 ■ Open Apr–Oct: 10am–5pm (Nov–Mar: to 3pm Wed–Fri, 5pm Sat & Sun) ■ Adm ■ www.glasgowsciencecentre.org

Housed in a landmark building, three floors of hands-on experiments puzzle and delight with miraculous science. There's an IMAX screen and the world's first revolving tower.

8 The Den & The Glen

MAP D6 ■ Maryculter, nr Aberdeen ■ (01224) 732 941 ■ Open 9:30am–5:30pm daily (last entry 4:30pm) ■ Adm ■ www.denandtheglen.co.uk

A family theme park with giant-sized models of nursery rhyme and story-book characters for kids to explore and enter make-believe worlds. Humpty Dumpty, Pooh and Postman Pat are among those present and there's a good indoor play area too known as the Den.

9 Scottish Seabird Centre

Zoom in on the wildlife of the Firth of Forth islands (the Bass Rock, Craigleith, Fidra and the Isle of May) using the interactive live cameras without disturbing them here (see p88). See gannets, kittiwakes, razorbills, guillemots, cormorants, puffins and, between October and December, grey seals with their pups. There have been sightings of bottlenose dolphins, porpoises and even whales. The centre also offers boat trips to the Bass Rock or Isle of May.

Gannet, Bass Rock

10 Beach Leisure Centre

MAP D6 ■ Beach Promenade, Aberdeen ■ (01224) 507 739 ■ Open daily (flume times vary) ■ Adm

Aberdeen has several swimming pools, but this is the one for flumes. There's a mini-flume for tots, but older children will be after the hairiest and scariest: the Pipeline, Wipeout and Tube. The last of these you ride on a tyre, while as for the other two … just close your eyes and hope for the best.

🔟 Whisky Distilleries

Whisky barrels at Springbank

1 Springbank

MAP G2 ■ Campbeltown ■ (01586) 552 009 ■ Adm ■ www.springbank.scot

Campbeltown was once a whisky smuggling centre, and the Springbank distillery, which dates back to 1828, was built on the site of an illicit still. This independent, family-owned business produces three distinctive malts – Springbank, Longrow and Hazelburn – and offers a choice of tours and tastings.

2 Glenlivet

MAP D5 ■ Ballindalloch ■ (01340) 821 720 ■ Open Mar–early Nov: 9am–6pm daily (last entry 4:30pm) ■ www.theglenlivet.com

One of the first distilleries to be legalized in 1824, the Glenlivet has been at the forefront of the industry ever since. A comprehensive tour includes the musty warehouse where the whisky ages for 12 to 18 years.

3 Laphroaig

MAP G2 ■ Nr Port Ellen, Islay ■ (01496) 302 418 ■ Various tours available; check tour timings ■ Adm ■ www.laphroaig.com

With their heavy smoked-peat flavour, the Islay malts really are in a class of their own. Even if you think you won't like them, try them! This malt is pronounced "la-froyg", but in truth your pronunciation doesn't matter – the taste is famous enough for instant recognition. A delightfully informal and intimate tour with plenty of wit and grist at a fine sea-edge location.

4 Talisker

MAP D2 ■ (01478) 614 308 ■ Adm ■ www.malts.com

The only distillery (see p27) on Skye and it's been producing a highly respected malt since 1830. Lively, informative tours last 40 minutes. Tours are organized all through the year but are less frequent in winter. Make sure to book ahead in summer.

5 Lagavulin

MAP G2 ■ Port Ellen, Islay ■ (01496) 302 749 ■ Check for tour timings ■ Adm ■ www.malts.com

Like its rival Laphroaig, this is a distinctive malt. Lagavulin whisky is made in a traditional distillery with unusual pear-shaped stills. The tour is highly personal and free of mass-market hustle.

Lagavulin distillery

LAGAVULIN

greats), but the best tour. Maybe because they're so remote, they try harder. Prepare to be taken through deep piles of malt drying in a delicious reek of peat.

9 Cardhu
MAP D5 ▪ Knockando ▪ (01479) 874 635 ▪ Check for tour timings ▪ Adm ▪ www.malts.com

The only distillery to have been pioneered by a woman and, aside from producing a distinguished single malt, it provides the heart of the Johnnie Walker blend. This is one of the smaller distilleries that has a range of tours, all offering a taste of Cardhu.

10 Macallan
MAP D5 ▪ Craigellachie ▪ (01340) 318 000 ▪ Open Easter–Sep: 9:30am–6pm Mon–Sat (Oct–Easter: to 5pm Mon–Fri) ▪ Adm ▪ www.themacallan.com

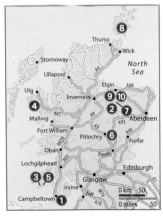

Macallan's whisky

Macallan is another of the famous Speyside brands, and the distillery boasts one of the most modern visitor centres in the valley. Aside from a guided tour, you explore whisky-making using the latest interactive technology. You can become a connoisseur by prearranging an individually tutored nosing and tasting tour.

Copper sills, Edradour distillery

6 Edradour
MAP E5 ▪ Nr Pitlochry ▪ (01796) 472 095 ▪ Tours mid-Apr–mid-Oct: Mon–Sat ▪ Adm ▪ www.edradour.com

Established in 1825, this is Scotland's smallest distillery and its cluster of buildings has remained virtually unchanged since the 1860s. To witness the process here is all the more delightful for its being in miniature. Only 12 casks a week are produced, making the screigh (as they say) "a rare treat for a few".

7 Glenfarclas
MAP D5 ▪ Ballindalloch ▪ (01807) 500 345 ▪ Open Oct–Mar & Apr–Sep: Mon–Fri; Jul–Sep: Sat; check for tour timings ▪ Adm ▪ www.glenfarclas.com

One of the few independent companies and justly proud of it. Established in 1836, this distillery is still owned and managed by the fifth generation of the Grant family. Tour the gleaming copper stills and then finish off by taking a dram in the splendid Ships Room.

8 Highland Park
MAP A5 ▪ Nr Kirkwall, Orkney ▪ (01856) 874 619 ▪ Tours: Apr–Oct daily; Nov–Mar Mon–Fri ▪ Adm ▪ www.highlandparkwhisky.com

Not the most famous whisky (though definitely among the

TOP10 Places to Eat

Romantic interiors of The Witchery by the Castle

1 The Witchery by the Castle

Tucked away at the top of the Royal Mile, by Edinburgh Castle, it is hard to beat this restaurant *(see p81)* for its sheer theatricality and romantic appeal. The Secret Garden, enclosed in a courtyard, boasts a painted ceiling and a quiet terrace, while the main dining room is oak-panelled and full of rich tapestries.

2 Brian Maule at Chardon d'Or

Set in a Victorian townhouse with polished wooden floors, fresh flowers and candles in the evening, this is one of Glasgow's finest restaurants *(see p101)*. Top quality beef, lamb and scallops, sourced from local suppliers, is prepared using French techniques. The menu features dishes such as rabbit roulade with roasted hazelnuts, grilled seabream with purple kale, and apple *tarte tatin* (caramelised fruit tart) with ice cream.

Delicious dessert at The Peat Inn

3 Braidwoods

This restaurant *(see p89)* first gained a Michelin star over 20 years ago and has impressed ever since.

Housed in a whitewashed cottage in the Ayrshire countryside, it offers roast loin of local lamb, or grilled fillet of turbot and monkfish. Book in advance.

4 The Cellar

Located in the fishing village of Anstruther, fresh fish is a speciality at this small, Michelin-starred eatery *(see p95)*. They offer a set menu and do not cater for vegan diets. Advance booking is essential.

5 The Peat Inn

Situated a short drive from the historic university town of St Andrews, this hotel's restaurant *(see p95)* is one of the most enduring and highly acclaimed places to eat in Scotland. Local produce is cooked in modern Scottish style. The menu includes roe deer with smoked swede puree, savoy cabbage, haggis and Madeira sauce.

6 The Kitchin

Run by celebrity chef Tom Kitchin, this restaurant *(see p81)* is set in a converted warehouse in Edinburgh's former docks. Scottish seasonal produce is lovingly prepared. There is even a creative vegetarian menu that features dishes such as sea kale salad and wild garlic and parsley risotto.

7 Three Chimneys

This iconic restaurant (see p127) in Skye, serves dishes designed to celebrate Scotland's culinary heritage. In addition to their main dining room, they have a "kitchen table" where guests can observe the chefs at work. It can seat eight people and can be reserved for exclusive use.

8 Knockinaam Lodge

Perched by the sea in Galloway, this acclaimed countryhouse hotel (see p89) offers gourmet dining. Expect some surprising combinations on the menu, such as roast chicken with a chicken and tarragon ravioli, mushroom puree and a cardamom and soya emulsion. Desserts might include a hot pistachio souffle with chocolate sauce.

Exterior of the Kinloch Lodge Hotel

9 Kinloch Lodge Hotel

It would be hard to beat this hotel's (see p127) idyllic setting, close to the water's edge in Sleat on the Isle of Skye. The food is equally delightful. The seven course tasting menu might feature Shetland cod with salt-baked beetroot.

10 The Silver Darling

Panoramic views of Aberdeen's beach are an attraction at this popular quayside restaurant (see p113). Scottish fish and shellfish are celebrated, with the menu featuring Shetland scallops, Loch Duart salmon and haddock from the North Sea.

TOP 10 SCOTTISH DISHES

Succulent venison ribs

1 Venison
The meat of wild red deer, dark and full-flavoured. It's served as a steak or cut into collops (slices of roast meat).

2 Haggis
Scotland's most famous dish is like a large, round sausage containing spiced sheep's offal, oats and seasoning. It is traditionally eaten at a Burn's supper with mashed "neeps" (swedes), "tatties" (potatoes) and a dram of whisky.

3 Grouse
One of Scotland's prized game birds, this dark meat is roasted and served with homemade bread sauce.

4 Stovies
A mix of potatoes, onions and beef cooked in the dripping (fat) from the Sunday roast.

5 Kippers
Fresh herring split open, salted and smoked. A common breakfast dish.

6 Arbroath Smokies
Similar to kippers, but these are smoked haddock rather than herring.

7 Smoked Salmon
Thin boneless slices of salmon that have been smoked to give a rich taste and deep pink colour.

8 Scotch Broth
A light soup made from mutton or beef stock, pearl barley and various vegetables such as carrots and leeks.

9 Cock-a-Leekie Soup
A warm, chunky soup of chicken, leeks, rice and prunes cooked in chicken stock – as wonderful as its name.

10 Cullen Skink
A Scottish version of chowder, this is a delicious soup made from smoked haddock, milk and mashed potato.

🔟 Scotland for Free

Scottish Parliament building, Edinburgh

1 Top Museums
All city museums in Glasgow and Edinburgh are free, so you won't have to pay to see many of the country's highlights, such as the National Museum of Scotland (see pp18–19), the Scottish National Gallery (see pp16–17) and Kelvingrove Art Gallery and Museum (see pp20–21).

2 Free Festival
www.freefestival.co.uk
Don't worry if you can't afford tickets to events in the Edinburgh Festival: the city is full of street performers in August, so just stroll around and enjoy the show. There is a free fringe programme too.

3 Holy Orders
Most of Scotland's churches are free to visit, including the historic St Giles' Cathedral in Edinburgh (see p14) and Glasgow Cathedral (see p97), though donations are welcome. Other churches include St Machar's Cathedral in Aberdeen.

4 Seat of Power
Scotland's increasingly powerful Parliament (see p15) sits in a striking contemporary building at the foot of Edinburgh's Royal Mile. You can visit for a free guided tour (book in advance), which lasts for an hour and includes details about the architecture as well as the history of the Scottish Parliament. Book a free ticket to attend First Minister's Question Time.

5 The Picts
MAP E5 ▪ Aberlemno
The Picts left few visible reminders of their presence in Scotland, except for their mysterious carved stones and crosses. View some in the area around Aberlemno, a short drive north of Glamis.

Pictish carved stone

6 Wild at Heart
St Abbs Head National Nature Reserve, Eyemouth: (01890) 771 443; www.nts.org.uk ▪ Scottish Dolphin Centre, Spey Bay: (01343) 820 339; open Apr–Oct: 10:30am–5pm; www.dolphincentre.whales.org
Scotland's wildlife is rich and varied, and it doesn't have to cost you a penny to see it. St Abbs Head National Nature Reserve is free and offers the chance to spot seabirds such as guillemots, kittiwakes and razorbills. At the Scottish Dolphin Centre you can enjoy land-based dolphin watching, hourly from 11am to 5pm.

Stained glass, St Giles' Cathedral

7 Glorious Garden

Entry is free to Glasgow's glorious Botanic Gardens (see p49), which offer riverside walks and an arboretum, as well as stunning Victorian glasshouses, the most famous of which is the Kibble Palace (see p99). There are fascinating guided walks in the summer.

8 Island Gin
www.lussagin.com

You can take a free tour of the wonderfully remote Lussa Gin Distillery on Jura. The gin is made using local botanicals such as bog myrtle and lemon thyme. Advance booking is recommended.

9 Ancient Trees

Scotland boasts some mighty trees that you can see for free. The most famous are the Birnam Oak in Dunkeld (see p94), said to be the last survivor of Birnam Wood mentioned in Shakespeare's *Macbeth*; and the 3,000-year-old Fortingall Yew in Fortingall's churchyard – a contender for Britain's oldest tree, a short drive west of Pitlochry (see p93).

The Birnam Oak, Dunkeld

10 Salmon Leap
MAP E4–5 ■ Pitlochry

On the Tummel in Pitlochry, you can watch salmon leaping up the specially constructed fish ladder, which bypasses a hydroelectric power station and allows thousands of fish to complete their annual migration.

TOP 10 BUDGET TIPS

Road bridge to the Isle of Skye

1 Getting to the Isle
Use the free road bridge rather than the ferry to reach Skye.

2 Historic Scotland Explorer Passes
www.historicenvironment.scot
For five or fourteen days, gives free entry to over 70 properties.

3 VAT Refund
Non-EU visitors can reclaim the 20 per cent Value Added Tax (VAT) at participating stores.

4 National Trust for Scotland
www.nts.org.uk
Membership provides free entry to over 100 of their properties.

5 Spirit of Scotland Pass
www.britrail.net
A four- or eight-day Spirit of Scotland Pass gives free travel on railways and many ferries.

6 Cairngorms Golf Pass
www.visitcairngorms.com
A pass provides 30 per cent off green fees at any of 12 courses.

7 Stay in a B&B
Book a B&B instead of a hotel – it is cheaper and will allow you to connect with locals who can offer travel tips.

8 Lunch It
Make lunch your main meal. Many top-tier (pricey) restaurants do great-value set menu lunches.

9 Sandemans New Europe
www.newedinburghtours.com
Sandemans offers free 2.5-hour walking tours of Edinburgh.

10 Itison
www.itison.com
An active online market for daily deals on accommodation, restaurant meals and activities. Check regularly, or subscribe.

🔟 Cultural Events

Performer playing a guitar at the Celtic Connections festival

① Celtic Connections
Venues throughout Glasgow ▪ Mid-Jan–late Jan ▪ (0141) 353 8000 ▪ www.celticconnections.com

The world's largest festival of Celtic music and culture, with performers from as far afield as Mongolia and the Cape Verde islands, as well as the Scots and Irish.

② Edinburgh International Science Festival
Early to mid-Apr ▪ (0131) 553 0320 ▪ www.sciencefestival.co.uk

Successfully combining education with entertainment in venues right across the city. There are exhibitions of the latest scientific advances, demonstrations of tomorrow's gadgets and serious debates.

③ Shetland Folk Festival
Shetland ▪ Early May ▪ (01595) 694 757 ▪ www.shetlandfolkfestival.com

These islands are the heartland of Scottish fiddle-playing, and this festival not only showcases the prodigious home-grown talent but also attracts the best from far afield.

④ Lanimer Day
MAP G4 ▪ Lanark ▪ Early/mid–Jun ▪ www.lanarklanimers.co.uk

Based on the annual custom of walking the town's boundaries (which started in 1140), this festival has developed into a week of fun events and fairground thrills. The highlight is the long parade of decorated floats, usually covered in thousands of paper flowers, and children dressed in outlandish costumes. A great community atmosphere prevails.

⑤ Edinburgh International Film Festival
MAP L4 ▪ Filmhouse ▪ Mid-Jun–late Jun ▪ (0131) 228 4051 ▪ www.edfilmfest.org.uk

Established in 1947, the festival now comprises four categories: world premieres, young British talent, film study and a major retrospective.

⑥ St Magnus Festival
MAP A5 ▪ Orkney ▪ Late Jun ▪ (01856) 871 445 ▪ www.stmagnusfestival.com

The Orkney islands have worked hard to create a cultural festival of exceptional quality. Events usually include at least one world premiere of either music or drama, and some of the world's best musicians. Timed to coincide with midsummer, the festival uses the remarkable island landscape to striking effect.

⑦ Glasgow Jazz Festival
End of Jun ▪ (08444) 539 027 ▪ www.jazzfest.co.uk

A jamboree that swamps the city with devotees of jazz and supplies top international musicians. Venues range from theatres to pubs, clubs and ad hoc stages.

⑧ T in the Park
MAP F5 ■ **Mid-Jul** ■ **www.tin thepark.com**

Sponsored by the Tennent's brewery, this is Scotland's biggest annual rock concert. The fields of Kinross are smothered in tents, while the bands get to perform in a giant castle of a marquee. Book in advance.

⑨ Edinburgh International Festival, Fringe and Military Tattoo
Festival: Aug; (0131) 473 2000; www. eif.co.uk ■ **Fringe: 5–29 Aug (approx); (0131) 226 0026; www.edfringe.com** ■ **Tattoo: 5–27 Aug (approx); (0131) 225 1188; www.edintattoo.co.uk**

The greatest extravaganza of music, drama, dance and opera on the planet. The Festival features the world's most prestigious performers, while the thousand-show Fringe brings the unknown and avant-garde. The massive spectacle of the castle's Military Tattoo parade is a swelling moment of national pride and vitality – a highly charged affair.

Edinburgh Fringe Festival

⑩ Edinburgh International Book Festival
MAP L3 ■ **Mid-Aug–late Aug (approx)** ■ **(0845) 373 5888** ■ **www.edbook fest.co.uk**

Charlotte Square plays host to this annual showcase of literary talent. It features best-selling authors for readings, debates and book signings.

TOP 10 RIOTOUS EVENTS

Up Helly Aa, Shetland

1 The Ba', Kirkwall
Wild ball game and free-for-all played in the town's crowded streets (Kirkwall, Orkney, 1 Jan).

2 Up Helly Aa
An incredible fire festival. Men dress as Vikings and burn a replica longboat (late Jan, Shetland).

3 Borders Rugby Sevens
Skill, passion and mud. In rugby's heartland, each border town takes a day as host (Apr/May).

4 Burns An' A' That!
Scotland's top musical talent celebrates Scottish culture at venues around Ayrshire (late May).

5 Royal Highland Show
Over 150,000 people celebrate the biggest, best and most cultivated in the farming world (Jun, Edinburgh).

6 Pride Edinburgh
Scotland's national LGBT+ festival, with a traditional march through the city (mid-Jun).

7 Edinburgh International Jazz & Blues Festival
A rival to Glasgow's, this is the capital's own festival of cool music with venues across the city (Jul).

8 Speyfest
The best folk and traditional music performers gather at Fochabers, which is between Elgin and Buckie (late Jul).

9 World Pipe Band Championships
Astonishing sights and sounds as 3,000 pipers from around the world play on Glasgow Green (mid-Aug).

10 Hogmanay, Edinburgh
Scotland's New Year's Eve. Crowds pack Princes Street (ticket only) and the castle is lit up by fireworks (31 Dec).

🔟 Island Attractions

Skara Brae, Orkney

producing its distinctive peat-smoked whisky. Now there are just eight distilleries (with the possibilty of more opening). The oldest, Bowmore, was first mentioned in 1779; the others are Ardbeg, Bruichladdich, Caol Ila, Bunnahbhain, Lagavulin, Laphroaig, and Kilchoman.

① Skara Brae, Orkney

The best-preserved group of prehistoric dwellings in Western Europe, this semi-subterranean village *(see p130)* is 5,000 years old and pre-dates the pyramids or Stonehenge. The nine houses were linked by covered passageways and you can see their "fitted" stone furniture. Artifacts such as gaming dice and jewellery are displayed in the visitor centre.

② Maeshowe, Orkney

It looks like just a grassy mound from the outside, but stoop low and walk along its narrow entrance passage and you find yourself in a stunning, 5,000-year-old chambered grave *(see p130)*. After years of use it was closed, then rediscovered by Norse invaders – who left runic graffiti on the walls.

③ Islay's Distilleries

MAP G2–F2 ■ www.islayinfo.com

They say that Irish monks introduced distilling to Islay in the 14th century. At one time there were over 20 distilleries on the island,

④ Iona Abbey and Nunnery

MAP F2 ■ (01681) 700 512 ■ Open Apr–Sep: 9:30am–5:30pm Mon–Sat (Oct–Mar: to 4pm) ■ Adm ■ www.historicenvironment.scot; www.welcometoiona.com

Iona has been a centre of Christian worship since AD 563, when St Columba founded his monastery here. It has been a pilgrimage site for hundreds of years. St Columba's shrine can be seen, as well as the 13th-century abbey church, and 8th-century stone crosses. It is said that Scottish kings and clan chiefs were buried here.

⑤ Fingal's Cave, Staffa

MAP E2 ■ (01681) 700 659; www.nts.org.uk ■ (01681) 700 755; www.staffatrips.co.uk

An Uamh Binn, or Cave of Melody, Fingal's Cave is a spectacular sea cave on the uninhabited island of Staffa. Its giant hexagonal columns and mystical beauty inspired Mendelssohn's *Hebrides Overture*, and featured in a painting by J M W Turner. Take a boat trip and see the island's fantastic wildlife such as basking sharks, seals and puffins.

Fingal's Cave, Staffa

6 The Italian Chapel, Orkney

MAP A5 ■ (01856) 781580 ■ Open Jun–Aug: 9am–6:30pm daily (May & Sep: to 5pm); Nov–Mar: 10am–1pm daily (Apr & Oct: to 4pm Mon–Sat, 3pm Sun) ■ Adm

Created from two Nissen huts by Domenico Chiocchetti and his fellow Italian prisoners of war between 1943 and 1944, this church is their memorial. Inside is trompe l'oeil brickwork and an altar made from scrap; painted glass windows depict St Francis of Assisi. Truly a labour of love.

The Italian Chapel

7 Kinloch Lodge, Skye

Lovely atmosphere at the home of Godfrey MacDonald, the chief of the MacDonald clan (see p43), and his wife Claire, an acclaimed cookery writer. Bedrooms are individually furnished, there are comfy sofas, log fires, and fine food in the restaurant (see p127). There's a cookery school, too.

8 Arran's Food Trail

MAP G3 ■ www.visitarran.com, www.taste-of-arran.co.uk

The Isle of Arran (see p126) produces a wonderful selection of food and drink. Put together your own island food trail by checking out its local oatcakes, ice cream, haggis, black pudding, cheeses, chocolate, whisky, beer, smoked fish, preserves and tablet (a bit like fudge, only harder and sweeter).

9 Calanais Standing Stones, Lewis

MAP B2 ■ (01851) 621422 ■ www.historic-scotland.gov.uk, www.calanaisvisitorcentre.co.uk

These magnificent stones, arranged in a cross shape with a central circle, were erected around 5,000 years ago. Later, a chambered tomb was added. Probably built as an astronomical observatory by a religious cult, they were abandoned around 1,000 years later. There's an informative exhibition in the visitor centre (check the website for opening hours).

Classic façade of the Isle of Eriska Hotel

10 Isle of Eriska Hotel

Get away at this sumptuous hotel (see p148), housed in a baronial castle and located on the tiny island of Eriska. On the grounds is a golf course and driving range, a croquet lawn, a spa, a swimming pool, a Michelin-starred restaurant and local wildlife. In addition to hotel rooms, there self-catering lodges, as well as spa suites set in private gardens. Dogs are welcome and special meals are available for them.

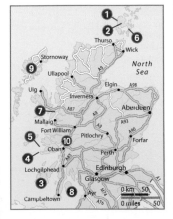

Scotland
Area by Area

The Dugald Stewart Monument
on top of Calton Hill, Edinburgh

⁞TOP⁞10 Edinburgh

National Museum of Scotland

With 18 golf courses, a dozen major parks, sufficient Neo-Classical architecture to dub it "the Athens of the North" and the crowning splendour of its castle, Edinburgh ranks as one of the world's most beautiful cities. Its centre is split in two: the historic Old Town, with its cobblestones and narrow wynds (alleys); and the striking Georgian architecture of the New Town. Between them lies Princes Street Gardens, a bowl of greenery in the heart of the bustle. No other city crams in as many festivals during the year as Edinburgh, and in August it becomes the greatest showcase on earth for comedy, music, drama, dance and every other conceivable form of culture.

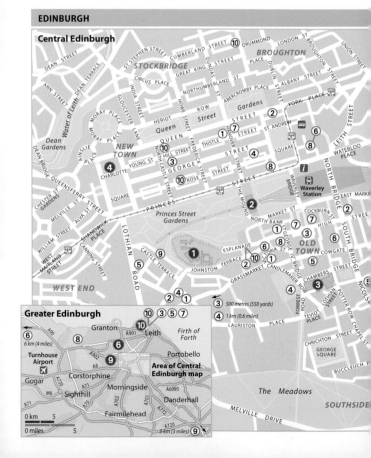

Edinburgh Castle on Castle Rock

① Edinburgh Castle and the Royal Mile

This world-famous castle *(see pp12–13)* wears the nation's history. Here you'll find the Scottish Crown, Sword and Sceptre, and the legendary Stone of Destiny. The Royal Mile *(see pp14–15)* treads a straight but diverting path from the castle to Holyroodhouse.

② Scottish National Gallery

Scotland's leading gallery *(see pp16–17)* includes masterpieces by the great Scottish artists, such as Raeburn and Ramsay, but is best known for its 15th- to 18th-century British and European paintings. In these collections, you'll find works by Botticelli, Velázquez, Raphael, Rembrandt, Rubens, Titian and many more besides.

③ National Museum of Scotland

Two adjoining buildings *(see pp18–19)* in radically different styles and with very diverse contents present the nation's most treasured historical artifacts. Worth visiting for the Lewis Chess Pieces alone, but don't expect to escape in under four hours.

④ Georgian House

MAP L3 ■ 7 Charlotte Square ■ 0131 225 2160 ■ Open Mar–Oct: 10am–5pm; Nov, Dec & Mar: 11am–4pm ■ Adm ■ www.nts.org.uk

A restored mansion on Charlotte Square, this is the best place to start a walking tour of the New Town. The area was the first daring adventure into planned architecture at a time of sordid living conditions for the masses. Begun in 1776, the beautifully proportioned buildings, set out in wide streets, crescents and squares, have lost none of their grandeur. Simply wander.

Map labels: MONTGOMERY ST, LEOPOLD PL, ⑨, HILLSIDE CRESCENT, LONDON ROAD, ROYAL TERRACE, CALTON, Regent Gardens, ⑧, REGENT TERRACE, ROAD, ABBEY HILL, CALTON ROAD, NEW STREET, ST MARY'S ST, CANONGATE, HOLYROOD ROAD, HORSE WYND, QUEEN'S DRIVE, ⑦, ⑤, COWGATE, PLEASANCE, Holyrood Park, Salisbury Crag, DUMBIEDYKES, LEONARD'S STREET, CLERK STREET, BUCCLEUCH STREET

0 metres 250
0 yards 250

① Top 10 Sights
see pp75–7

① Places to Eat
see p81

① Bars and Pubs
see p80

① Places to Shop
see p79

① The Best of the Rest
see p78

Bedroom at Georgian House

5 Our Dynamic Earth
MAP R3 ▪ Holyrood Rd ▪ (0131)
550 7800 ▪ Open Feb–Oct: 10am–
5:30pm daily (Jul & Aug: to 6pm)
▪ Adm ▪ www.dynamicearth.co.uk

Every bit as exciting and illuminating
for adults as it is for kids, Our
Dynamic Earth (see p60) takes you on
a journey through time and tells the
story of planet Earth, from the Big
Bang to the present. Amid this rapid
evolution, environmental concerns
are brought to the fore.

6 Royal Botanic Garden
MAP K5 ▪ 20a Inverleith
Row, Edinburgh ▪ (0131) 552 7171
▪ Open Mar–Sep: 10am–6pm daily
(Feb & Oct: to 5pm; Nov & Jan: to
4pm) ▪ Adm for glasshouses
▪ www.rbge.org.uk

Scotland's premier garden (see p48)
with species from around the world.
The guided tours will feed a curiosity
you won't have realized you had.

7 Holyroodhouse
Originally the abbey
guesthouse, this was turned into a
royal palace (see p15) by James IV of
Scotland and is the Queen's official
Scottish residence; she visits each
summer. The Queen's Gallery is lined
with portraits of Scottish royalty. The
Royal Apartments are associated with
Mary, Queen of Scots: it was here
that David Rizzio, her Italian secre-
tary, was brutally murdered on
the orders of her husband,
Lord Darnley. The Queen

PRINCES STREET GARDENS

An area of neutrality between New
Town and Old, these lovely gardens
shelter under the wing of the clifftop
castle. During the Festival they become
a major events venue, and throughout
summer the famous Floral Clock, com-
prising over 2,000 plants, blooms in
a corner by The Mound.

meets ministers and dignitaries
in the State Apartments and the
Throne Room is used for receptions
and State occasions. In 1745, Bonnie
Prince Charlie held extravagant
balls in the Great Gallery and set
up court in the palace for six weeks.

8 Calton Hill
MAP P2

Rising above the New Town with
fantastic views, Calton Hill is home
to a gathering of Classical buildings:
the columned National Monument
for the dead of the Napoleonic Wars,
the Nelson Monument, commem-
orating the Battle of
Trafalgar and the Old
City Observatory.

Holyroodhouse

Visitors viewing modern art exhibits

9 Scottish National Gallery of Modern Art

MAP J3 ■ 75 Belford Rd ■ Open 10am–5pm daily (Aug: to 6pm) ■ www.nationalgalleries.org

Since it opened in 1960, this gallery has amassed some 5,000 post-1890 works. Here you can find the hand of such diverse figures as Picasso, Munch, Charles Rennie Mackintosh and the Pop Art trio of Richard Hamilton, David Hockney and Jake Tilson. Also check out Modern Two opposite for contemporary shows.

The grand royal yacht *Britannia*

10 Royal Yacht Britannia

MAP K5 ■ Ocean Terminal, Leith ■ (0131) 555 5566 ■ Open Apr–Oct: 9:30am– 4:30pm daily; Nov–Mar: 10am– 3:30pm daily ■ Adm ■ www.royalyachtbritannia. co.uk

From 1953 to 1997 this was the Queen's floating home, the honeymooning hotel of her children and Britain's roving royal court. Wander the decks of this fabulous ship with an audio tour that tells of the life and times of *Britannia*.

A DAY IN EDINBURGH

▶ MORNING

Start at the **Scottish National Gallery** (see pp16–17) at 10am. Ninety minutes should allow you to see the Botticelli, Canova and Raeburn's skating minister, the Rev Robert Walker, and far more.

Enter **Princes Street Gardens** at the Floral Clock (opposite the gallery), and ascend the path to **Edinburgh Castle** (see pp12–13), taking care, as it's a steep climb.

Tour the castle, keeping an eye on your watch to make sure you're present when the dramatic One O'Clock Gun goes off. At the **Redcoat Café** (Map M4; (0131) 225 9746; www.edinburghcastle.scot), have a platter to restore your energy levels before soldiering on.

AFTERNOON

Stroll down from the Castle Esplanade to the **Royal Mile** (see pp14–15), stopping off at the St Giles' Cathedral (see p14) and probably several shops as well. Admire **John Knox's House** and have hot chocolate in **The Elephant House** (Map N4; 21 George IV Bridge; (0131) 220 5355) where the first of the Harry Potter books was written.

Turn right off the Royal Mile at Reid's Close (easy to miss) and visit **Our Dynamic Earth**, where you can pass several million years in a mere 2 hours or so.

If you still feel energetic, walk up the Salisbury Crags and **Arthur's Seat** for great evening views. Ninety minutes up and down (if you're fit) or grab a taxi and be driven most of the way up.

See map on pp74–5

The Best of the Rest

1 The Writers' Museum

Celebrating three great Scottish writers, Burns, Scott and Stevenson, The Writers' Museum *(see p14)* has rare books and items such as Burns' writing desk. There is Stevenson's wardrobe, made by the infamous Deacon Brodie, who was the inspiration behind *The Strange Case of Dr Jekyll and Mr Hyde*.

The Writers' Museum sign

2 Scottish National Portrait Gallery

MAP N2 ■ Queen St
■ www.nationalgalleries.org

Marvel at over 3,000 portraits of famous Scots, including Robert Burns and Bonnie Prince Charlie.

3 St Giles' Cathedral

The Scottish Reformation was launched by John Knox in this church *(see p14)*. Attractions include the Thistle Chapel and memorials to Robert Burns and Robert Louis Stevenson. There are guided rooftop tours on weekends.

4 Greyfriars Kirk

MAP N4

Historic church, best known for its statue (in the street) of "Greyfriars Bobby" (1858–72), a devoted terrier who lived by his master's grave.

5 Surgeons' Hall Museum

MAP P4 ■ Nicolson St ■ (0131) 527 1711 ■ Adm ■ www.museum. rcsed.ac.uk

Appreciating Edinburgh's contribution to surgery. Sections cover midwifery, bodysnatching and war medicine, plus an exhibit on Sir Arthur Conan Doyle.

6 Hopetoun

MAP J5 ■ Sth Queensferry ■ (0131) 331 2451 ■ Adm ■ www.hopetoun.co.uk

This architectural gem built by the industrious Robert Adam, is both a stately home of the Earls of Hopetoun and an art treasury (paintings by Canaletto, Rubens, Rembrandt, to name but a few).

7 Real Mary King's Close

MAP N3 ■ 2 Warriston's Cl, High St ■ (0131) 225 0672 ■ Adm ■ www.realmarykingsclose.com

Shiver as you tour this warren of streets hidden beneath the City Chambers. Closed off after the 1645 plague, they are said to be haunted.

8 Lauriston Castle

Davidson's Mains ■ (0131) 336 2060 ■ Adm ■ www.edinburgh museums.org.uk

This Edwardian mansion boasts a 16th-century tower house, lovely grounds, and fine furniture and antiques. Admission by tour only.

9 Scottish Mining Museum

Newtongrange ■ (0131) 663 7519 ■ Adm ■ www.nationalmining museum.com

Don your headlamp for an enlightening underground tour.

10 Scotch Whisky Experience

MAP M4 ■ Castlehill ■ (0131) 220 0441 ■ Adm ■ www.scotchwhisky experience.co.uk

A replica distillery with the world's largest collection of Scotch whisky.

Places to Shop

1 Edinburgh Books
MAP M4 ■ 145 West Port
One of many independent bookshops, to the west of Grassmarket, sells new and second-hand books. West Port's selection focuses on the arts.

2 Hector Russell
MAP N3–4 ■ 137-141 High St
Made-to-measure kilts and a gathering of the tartans. They offer kilts for hire too.

3 Whistles
MAP M2 ■ 97 George St
This is one of several boutique fashion stores that have made George Street their home. They feature high fashion for women.

4 Halibut & Herring
MAP L6 ■ 108 Bruntsfield Place
Find Scottish handmade soaps here and all manner of colourful, squeezy and bathroom accessories, in aquatic hues. It is a useful stop to buy gifts.

5 Printmakers' Workshop
Castle Mills, 1 Dundee St
On display here are a range of limited-edition works from contemporary printmakers at reasonable prices.

6 Iain Mellis
MAP N4 ■ 30 Victoria St
Iain Mellis's cheeses are celebrated all around Scotland, and feature in many Edinburgh menus, but the Victoria Street branch goes beyond to embrace a panoply of culinary delicacies. Stock your picnic hamper here.

Scotch Whisky Experience, Royal Mile

7 Royal Mile Whiskies
MAP N4 ■ 379 High St
A cornucopia of all things alcoholic, particularly single malt Scotch whisky, with hundreds of varieties on offer and regular tasting sessions.

8 Jenners
MAP N3 ■ 47 Princes St
Founded in the 1830s, this is the oldest department store in the world, but only occupies its present site since 1895. Jenners sells a miscellany of high-quality goods, luxury as well as designer brands.

9 Edinburgh Farmers' Market
MAP L4 ■ Castle Terrace
The city's weekly foodie fest spreads its wares beneath the castle crags every Saturday morning, selling everything from Scottish cheeses and venison sandwiches, to local craft beers and traditional Scottish sweets.

10 Tiso Edinburgh
MAP M3 ■ 123 Rose St
■ Leith branch: 41 Commercial St
An outdoor clothing and gear shop, Tiso Edinburgh has everything you need before heading for the hills. The Leith branch also offers a café and a ski servicing centre.

Cheeses at Iain Mellis

See map on pp74–5

Bars and Pubs

1 Bow Bar
MAP N4 ■ 80 West Bow St
Lush red and cream gloss paintwork
envelops this modest pub, where the
background sounds are the jovial
chatter and clinking glasses.

2 The Blue Blazer
MAP L5 ■ 2 Spittal St
Perfect for discerning drinkers, this
place offers real ales and an array of
malt whiskies. The back room hosts
regular live folk-music sessions.

3 Bennet's
MAP L6 ■ 8 Leven St
Once ordinary, Bennet's pubness is
rapidly becoming exotic, and attracts
a mixed crowd. They serve drinks in
pint pots and cheap lunches.

4 Dome Bar
MAP M2 ■ 14 George St
Dome Bar is a Corinthian-columned
whale of a building, entered through
a flight of steps flanked by nocturnal
doormen. Its interiors are decorated
with chandeliers and palm plants.
There are many bars and dining
areas such as the Georgian Tea
Room and the majestic Grill Room.
The Front Bar is great for cocktails.

Lavish interior of Dome Bar

Craft beer bar, BrewDog

5 BrewDog
MAP N4 ■ 143 Cowgate
Scotland's most successful artisan
brewery operates this industrial-chic
altar to craft beer, a hugely popular
oasis of real ales in the Old Town.

6 City Café
MAP P4 ■ 19 Blair St
Ideally situated in the heart of the
city's clubland, this popular bar
packs in the capital's contingent of
party people on weekend nights.

7 Bramble
MAP M2 ■ 16a Queen St
Stone steps lead down to this
maze-like, candlelit cellar where
accomplished mixologists create
some of Edinburgh's finest cocktails.

8 Café Royal Circle Bar
MAP N2 ■ 19 West Register St
Walk in at lunchtime to swirling
ceilings, brass lamps and a convivial
atmosphere of both young and old,
enjoying simple seafood dishes from
the kitchen of the Oyster Bar next door.

9 Joseph Pearce
MAP P1 ■ 23 Elm Row,
Leith Walk
Swedish owners have taken this
century-old Scottish pub and given it
a Scandinavian makeover, creating a
welcoming and family-friendly bar.

10 The Cumberland
MAP M1 ■ 1–3 Cumberland St
Enjoy the well-lit, cozy interiors of this
much-loved pub in the winter, or cool
down in its side garden in the summer.

Places to Eat

PRICE CATEGORIES
For a three-course meal for one with half a bottle of wine (or equivalent meal), taxes and extra charges.

£ under £30 ££ £30–60 £££ over £60

1 **Henderson's**
MAP M2 ▪ 94 Hanover St ▪ (0131) 225 2131 ▪ £

Delicious wholesome cafeteria food is served in a bohemian setting at this vegetarian restaurant. There is live music every Friday evening.

2 **The Witchery by the Castle**
MAP M4 ▪ Castlehill ▪ (0131) 225 5613 ▪ ££

Aim for the Secret Garden room to experience The Witchery (see p64) at its romantic best. It excels at dishes with a rural flavour. Try the foraged soup, roast wood pigeon, loin of venison.

3 **Restaurant Martin Wishart**
MAP K5 ▪ 54 The Shore, Leith ▪ (0131) 553 3557 ▪ £££

Make sure to book ahead for this Michelin-starred restaurant. The food is memorable and the lunch is of excellent value.

4 **Timberyard**
MAP M4 ▪ 10 Lady Lawson St ▪ (0131) 221 1222 ▪ £££

Authenticity and originality are the watchwords at this beautifully converted woodworking shop. The focus is on locally produced seafood, pork and game garnished with foraged ingredients, such as damsons and mustard leaf.

5 **Fishers, Leith**
1 The Shore, Leith; (0131) 554 5666 ▪ Fishers in the City (sister restaurant): MAP M2; 58 Thistle St ▪ ££

This seafood restaurant is loved for its honed cooking and warm ambience.

6 **Hawksmoor**
MAP N2 ▪ The Balmoral, 1 Princes St ▪ (0131) 526 4790 ▪ ££

Located in the former National Bank of Scotland, this acclaimed restaurant specializes in beef as well as seafood dishes.

7 **The Kitchin**
MAP F5 ▪ 78 Commercial St ▪ (0131) 555 1755 ▪ £££

Tom Kitchin's restaurant (see p64) has made a startling impact on the country's culinary scene. Find out what makes this Leith outlet special by sampling some of the exemplary French-influenced cuisine here.

French cuisine, The Kitchin

8 **Ondine**
MAP N4 ▪ 2 George IV Bridge ▪ (0131) 226 1888 ▪ £££

Seafood, from Scottish lobster to Portuguese prawns via Breton shellfish, graces the menu at this sleek and sophisticated restaurant.

9 **Gardener's Cottage**
MAP Q1 ▪ 1 Royal Terrace Gdns, London Rd ▪ (0131) 677 0244 ▪ ££

Diners share communal tables in this cosy eatery, where the set menu changes daily with ingredients from the cottage's own organic garden.

10 **Le Café St-Honoré**
MAP M2 ▪ 34 North West Thistle St Lane ▪ (0131) 226 2211 ▪ £££

Bistro food that's both familiar and better than ever. A charmer!

See map on pp74–5

🔟 Southern Scotland

A beautiful region of abrupt and rolling hills, sheep pastures, forested valleys and slow-moving rivers, Southern Scotland is the home of rugby, Robert Burns, Sir Walter Scott and spectacular castles and abbeys. For centuries this border country was the flashpoint of hostility between Scotland and England, but also a centre of commerce and religion. The monuments of these times represent some of the best medieval and Renaissance architecture in Europe. Still sparsely inhabited, the border towns contest their rugby reputations in winter and, with equal passion, celebrate ancient riding festivals in summer.

Burns Monument, Alloway

SOUTHERN SCOTLAND

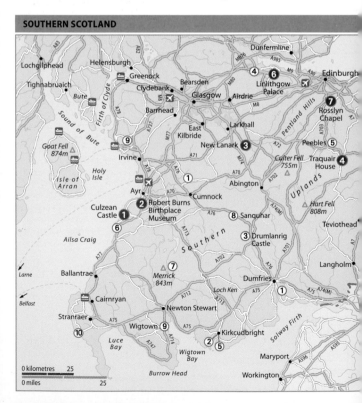

1 Culzean Castle

This cliff-edge castle (see pp32–3) was remodelled into a magnificent home for the Earls of Cassillis in 1777 by Georgian architectural master Robert Adam.

2 Robert Burns Birthplace Museum

MAP G4 ■ Murdoch's Lone, Alloway ■ (01292) 443 700 ■ Open 10am–5:30pm (cottage: 11am–5pm) ■ Adm (free for NTS members) ■ www.burns museum.org.uk

Scotland's most famous poet was born in this two-room cottage in Alloway, which is now a museum dedicated to his life and work. It houses the world's finest collection of Burns memorabilia and original manuscripts, including "Auld Lang Syne". The heritage park includes the Burns Monument.

New Lanark on the River Clyde

3 New Lanark

MAP G4 ■ (01555) 661 345 ■ Open Apr–Oct: 10am–5pm (Nov–Mar: to 4pm) ■ Adm ■ www.newlanark.org

In 1820, at the height of the Industrial Revolution, factory owner Robert Owen recognized the need for safe and efficient working conditions, matched by good-quality housing for his workers. New Lanark was the result, a modern industrial town that also boasted an education system (including the world's first nursery school) and free healthcare. Now a UNESCO World Heritage Site, this living museum is still pioneering.

4 Traquair House

MAP G5 ■ Innerleithen ■ (01896) 830 323 ■ Open Apr–Jun & Sep: 11am–5pm daily (Oct: to 4pm; Nov: to 3pm Sat & Sun); Jul & Aug: 10am–5pm ■ Adm ■ www.traquair.co.uk

Atmospheric Traquair dates back to 1107 and is Scotland's oldest inhabited house. The interior includes a hidden room leading to secret stairs along which Catholic priests could escape during persecutions. Bonnie Prince Charlie once stayed here.

5 Manderston House

MAP F6 ■ Duns ■ (01361) 883 450 ■ House: open May–Sep: 1:30–5pm Thu & Sun ■ Gardens: open 11:30am–dusk ■ Adm

This stunning Edwardian mansion, featuring a lake and woodland, covers a massive area and was built to impress Scottish society. The most lavish feature of the interior is the silver staircase; there are also fine artworks and antiques.

1 Top 10 Sights
see pp85–7

1 Places to Eat
see p89

1 The Best of the Rest
see p88

6 Linlithgow Palace

MAP F5 ■ Linlithgow
■ (01506) 842896
■ Open Apr–Sep:
9:30am–5:30pm
daily; Oct–Mar:
10am–4pm daily
■ Adm

One of only four royal
palaces in Scotland,
Linlithgow was the
birthplace of Mary
Queen of Scots and
provided a temporary
safe haven for Bonnie
Prince Charlie during

Mary Queen of Scots

the Jacobite Rebellion *(see p38)*.
Solid and fortress-like on the banks
of Linlithgow Loch, the palace still
looks majestic in its semi-ruined
state. This was the finest building
of its day, and its master masons
have left a wealth of carvings. Look
around the Great Hall and chapel
and marvel at the expertise of the
craftsmen who laboured upon this
wonderful building.

7 Rosslyn Chapel

MAP F5 ■ Rosslyn ■ (0131) 440
2159 ■ Open 9:30am–5pm Mon–Sat
(Jun–Aug: to 6pm), noon–4:45pm
Sun ■ Adm ■ www.rosslynchapel.com

As extraordinary as it is mysterious,
you'd be hard pushed to cram more
carvings into such a small place.
Built in 1446, it seems that every
master mason had to do a turn here,

Intricate carvings in Rosslyn Chapel

such is the variety of styles and
subjects. Most curious of all are the
carvings of New World plants. They
predate Columbus's transatlantic
voyage of discovery by 100 years.
The chapel has become extremely
popular since featuring in the book
and film *The Da Vinci Code*.

8 Melrose Abbey

MAP G5 ■ Melrose
■ (01896) 822562 ■ Open Apr–Sep:
9:30am–5:30pm daily; Oct–Mar:
10am–4pm daily ■ Adm

The tall lancet windows of this ruin
must have appeared miraculous to
medieval worshippers. Founded in
1136 by David I, this was the first
Cistercian monastery in Scotland.
It was rebuilt in the 1380s having
suffered due to border conflicts,
but faced further damage in the
16th century. It now stands as a
beleaguered but romantic spot for
the ghost of Robert the Bruce, whose
heart is believed to reside here.

Melrose Abbey

⑨ Mellerstain House
MAP G6 ▪ Gordon ▪ (01573) 410225 ▪ Open Easter & May late Sep: 12:30–5pm Fri–Mon ▪ Adm ▪ www.mellerstain.com

Scotland's most splendid Georgian house (early 18th century) is another creation by architect Robert Adam. A vast edifice of perfect symmetry on the outside contains rooms of perfect proportions within. The delicate plasterwork of the library, resembling fine china, is considered one of Adam's greatest accomplishments. Exquisite details abound throughout the interior, while outside, grand terraced gardens run down to an ornamental lake.

Façade of Mellerstain House

⑩ Dryburgh Abbey
MAP G6 ▪ Nr St Boswells ▪ (01835) 822381 ▪ Open Apr–Sep: 9:30am–5:30pm daily; Oct–Mar: 10am–4pm daily ▪ Adm (free for HES members) ▪ www.historicenvironment.scot

Located on a bend in the River Tweed, these are the most beautiful and evocative ruins in southern Scotland. Founded in 1152, the abbey was destroyed by the English in 1322, 1344 and again in 1385, but each time it rose to magnificence once more, until it was finally consumed by fire in 1544. Despite having lain in ruin for 500 years, it is remarkably complete, and the quality of masonry is unbelievable. See it when shadows fall for the most spectacular views.

A TOUR OF THE BORDERS

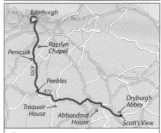

▶ MORNING

Shop at the **Edinburgh Farmers' Market** *(see p79)* or Iain Mellis the day before your trip to make a gourmet picnic – as simple or as lavish as you like.

The next morning, set off at 9am, just after rush hour, and drive to **Rosslyn Chapel** to see the extraordinary carvings. Tear yourself away from this magical spot, and drive on to Penicuik and take the A703 to Peebles. It's worth having a break for coffee in this pretty town.

Now take the lovely Tweedside A72, then bear off onto the B7062 to reach **Traquair House** *(see p85)*. Explore this fascinating building, which is still home to the Maxwell-Stuart family, then enjoy lunch at one of the picnic tables in the extensive grounds.

AFTERNOON

Return to the A72, then continue to visit either **Abbotsford House** *(see p88)*, the home of Sir Walter Scott, or drive a bit further to the romantic ruins of **Dryburgh Abbey**, where the great writer is buried. Both properties, which close about 5pm, are a short drive from Scott's View, from where you can see the Eildon Hills while you delve once more into your picnic hamper for afternoon tea.

Return to Edinburgh for your evening meal, or continue to explore the Borders at your leisure and enjoy the stunning scenery.

See map on pp84–5 ←

The Best of the Rest

The stunning Caerlaverock Castle

1 Caerlaverock Castle
MAP H5 ■ 13 km (8 miles) SE of Dumfries on the B725 ■ (01387) 770 244 ■ Adm (free for HES members) ■ www.historicenvironment.scot

This triangular castle within a moat makes a stunning sight. It is remarkably complete, despite having been ruined for over 400 years.

2 Abbotsford House
MAP G5 ■ Nr Melrose ■ (01896) 752 043 ■ Open Mar & Nov: 10am–4pm daily (Apr–Oct: to 5pm) ■ Adm ■ www.scottsabbotsford.com

Home of the great novelist Sir Walter Scott, crammed with historical bric-a-brac. A short drive away on the B6356 is Scott's View.

3 Drumlanrig Castle
MAP G4 ■ Thornhill, Dumfries and Galloway ■ (01848) 331 555 ■ Castle: open Jul, Aug, Easter and May: 11am–5pm on hols ■ Grounds: Apr–Sep: open 10am–5pm ■ Adm ■ www.drumlanrigcastle.co.uk

This lavish 1676 castle of turrets and domes is home to the Duke of Buccleuch. It's filled with treasures.

4 Falkirk Wheel
MAP F4 ■ Falkirk ■ (08700) 500 208 ■ Visitor centre: open 10am–5:30pm daily ■ Adm (for boat trips) ■ www.scottishcanals.co.uk

This engineering marvel is a "world's first"; revolving scoops connect two canal systems on different levels. Canal boats enter a giant "bucket", the wheel revolves and boats are moved. Visitors can take boat trips.

5 Kirkcudbright
MAP H4 ■ Dumfries and Galloway ■ www.kirkcudbright.town

Pronounced "kirkoobree", this town and artists' colony has a ruined castle and was home to artist E A Hornel. Buy locally made arts and crafts here.

6 Scottish Seabird Centre
MAP F5 ■ North Berwick ■ (01620) 890 202 ■ Open Apr–Aug: 10am–6pm daily; closes earlier rest of year ■ Adm ■ www.seabird.org

Remote cameras relay live action from the Bass Rock's 100,000 gannets. Take time for a boat trip (see p61).

7 Galloway Forest Park
MAP H4 ■ www.galloway forestpark.com

Area of superb loch, forest and hill scenery. Picnic at Bruce's Stone or have a day out on foot or on bikes.

8 St Abb's Head
MAP F6 ■ Visitor centre: (01890) 771 443; open Apr–Oct: 10am–5pm daily

A national nature reserve on dramatic cliffs packed with birds. Don't miss the characterful town of St Abb's with its fishery museum.

9 Wigtown
MAP H4 ■ www.wigtown-booktown.co.uk

Pretty market town that has become a "book town", full of all sorts of literary specialities and events.

10 Floors Castle
MAP G6 ■ Kelso ■ (01573) 223 333 ■ Open Easter–Apr & May–Sep: 10:30am–5pm daily (Oct: weekends only) ■ Adm ■ www.floorscastle.com

Get a real taste of Downton Abbey at this magnificent property built in 1721 for the first Duke of Roxburghe and still the family home.

Places to Eat

PRICE CATEGORIES

For a three-course meal for one with half a bottle of wine (or equivalent meal), taxes and extra charges.

£ under £30   ££ £30–60   £££ over £60

1 Sorn Inn
MAP G4 ▪ 25 Main St, Sorn, Ayrshire ▪ (01290) 551 305 ▪ ££

Family-friendly country pub serving quality classics like steak pie, roast chicken and haddock and chips.

2 The Castle Restaurant
MAP H4 ▪ 5 Castle St, Kirkcudbright ▪ (01557) 330 569 ▪ ££

The French-influenced cuisine at The Castle is created using organic ingredients whenever possible.

3 Cobbles Inn
MAP G6 ▪ 7 Bowmont St, Kelso ▪ (01573) 223 548 ▪ ££

Popular town-centre gastropub offering bar lunches, fine dining in the evening, and craft beers from the nearby Tempest microbrewery.

4 Wheatsheaf at Swinton
MAP G6 ▪ The Green, Swinton ▪ (01890) 860 257 ▪ ££

Local lamb, fish and game are on the menu at this smart, country-style restaurant with a lovely setting overlooking the village green.

5 Peebles Hydro
MAP G5 ▪ Innerleithen Rd, Peebles ▪ (01764) 651 846 ▪ ££

The changing menu at this restaurant features international and traditional dishes such as crusted cod loin and braised pork belly, with desserts such as pear and blackberry crumble.

6 Wildings Restaurant
MAP G4 ▪ Harbour Rd, Maidens, Ayrshire ▪ (01655) 331 401 ▪ ££

An attractive restaurant with Isle of Arran views. The seasonal menu uses local ingredients. Book ahead.

7 Marmions
MAP G5 ▪ Buccleuch St, Melrose ▪ (01896) 822 245 ▪ Closed Sun ▪ ££

Long-running French-style brasserie, popular with both locals and visitors. Snacks, an à la carte menu and wines for all tastes.

8 Blackaddie Country House Hotel
MAP G4 ▪ Sanquhar ▪ (01659) 50270 ▪ £££

A classy restaurant serving modern Scottish dishes made from quality local produce.

9 Braidwoods
MAP G4 ▪ Drumastle Mill Cottage, Dalry, Ayrshire ▪ (01294) 833 544 ▪ Closed Sun and Mon ▪ £££

Four- to six-week waits are an indication of the quality on offer. Braidwoods (see p64) fuses indigenous produce with a multicultural approach to a craft that takes in French and Italian influences.

10 Knockinaam Lodge
MAP H3 ▪ Portpatrick ▪ (01776) 810 471 ▪ £££

Traditional food with a modern touch in a sumptuous country house (see p65). Memorable seafood, such as a simple dish of pan seared scallops. A five-course tasting menu offers the best of the kitchen.

Picturesque Knockinaam Lodge

See map on pp84–5 ←

TOP 10 North and East of Edinburgh

A two-hour drive from the centre of Edinburgh takes you either into the majestic Highland-like landscape of Perthshire, or through the rich farmland of Fife, with its coastal fringe of pretty seaside villages.

Quaint cottages in Culross

This area is Scotland arguably at its most diverse, with famous castles, abbeys, ships, bridges, wildlife reserves and golf courses all found within easy reach of each other by car. Golf is Scotland's greatest sporting tradition, and it is much in evidence here – especially in St Andrews, the sport's spiritual home. The many castles and palaces are testament to the enduring appeal of this pleasing and photogenic region.

NORTH AND EAST OF EDINBURGH

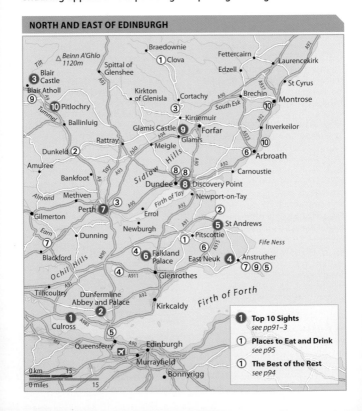

Top 10 Sights
see pp91–3

Places to Eat and Drink
see p95

The Best of the Rest
see p94

① Culross

MAP F5 ■ Palace: (01383) 880 359; open Apr–late Sep: 10am–5pm daily (Oct–late Mar: to 4pm Fri–Mon ■ Adm (free for NTS members) ■ www.nts.org.uk

Once a thriving village with mines, iron workings and trade links with the Low Countries, Culross fell into decline in the 18th and 19th centuries. Its restoration began in the 1930s, and now the town is a striking resurrection of its 16th- and 17th-century heyday.

② Dunfermline Abbey and Palace

MAP F5 ■ Dunfermline ■ (01383) 739 026 ■ Open Apr–late Sep: 9:30am–5pm daily; Oct–late Mar: 10am–4pm Sat–Wed ■ Adm ■ www.dunfermline abbey.co.uk

Founded in the 11th century by Queen (later St) Margaret (see p13), the abbey's stunning feature is the 12th-century Romanesque nave. This was the burial place of Robert the Bruce – without his heart, which he requested be taken on a Crusade to the Holy Land. A skeleton with the heart chamber cut open was discovered in a grave here in 1818; the site is now marked by a plaque to honour the hero of the Battle of Bannockburn (see p38).

③ Blair Castle

MAP E4 ■ Blair Atholl ■ (01796) 481 207 ■ Open Apr–Oct: 9:30am–5:30pm ■ Adm ■ www. blair-castle.co.uk

This striking castle is the ancestral seat of the Dukes of Atholl. Dating

Blair Castle and the hills of Perthshire

from 1269, it has been extended over the centuries and boasts crenellations, turrets and a grand ballroom. Queen Victoria was so impressed when she stayed that she gave the then Duke permission to raise a private army. You may see one of his Atholl Highlanders playing the bagpipes in summer.

④ East Neuk

MAP F5–6

Neuk is a Scots word for "corner", and the East Neuk refers to a small bend in the coastline along which is found a remarkable chain of picturesque fishing villages. They run from Earlsferry to Crail, and every one is a gem. Elie and Crail are probably the most quaint and are favoured haunts of artists. Pittenweem's beautiful harbour is still a working port, and Anstruther, a haven for yachts, has a bustling seafront. The Scottish Fisheries Museum (see p94) is excellent and worth a stop.

Yachts docked at the busy harbour in Anstruther

The ruins of St Andrews Cathedral

5 St Andrews

MAP F5 ▪ Cathedral & Castle: open Apr–Sep: 9:30am–5:30pm daily, Oct–Mar: 10am–4pm daily; adm ▪ Golf courses: (01334) 466 666; www.st andrews.org.uk

The "home of golf" *(see p56)* has the oldest university in Scotland, and red-robed students add a colourful, carefree atmosphere to this town. St Andrews was once the ecclesiastical capital of the country and its cathedral is still a proud ruin. Its castle has unrivalled examples of siege tunnels and a curious "bottle dungeon". There's also a long beach for walks, and plenty of hip cafés and bistros.

> **HOME OF GOLF**
>
> The coastal links courses around St Andrews are recognized as the birthplace of golf – the earliest record of the game being played here dates to 1457. Golfing heritage continues in the city to this day, and St Andrew's Royal and Ancient Golf Club remains the ruling arbiter of the game.

6 Falkland Palace

MAP F5 ▪ Falkland ▪ (0844) 493 2186 ▪ Open Mar–late May & Sep–late Oct: 11am–5pm Mon–Sat (Jun–late Aug: from 10am Mon–Sat, from noon Sun) ▪ Adm (free for NTS members) ▪ www.nts.org.uk

A sense of history pervades this palace, the home of Mary Queen of Scots and the Stuart kings from 1541. Restored royal bedchambers and fine 17th-century tapestries are on display. Most intriguing is the

Falkland Palace crest

oldest real tennis court still in use in Britain, built in 1539. Unlike the modern game, real tennis was played indoors and is similar to squash.

7 Perth and Scone Palace

MAP E5 ▪ Palace: (01738) 552 300; open May–Sep: 9:30am–5pm (Apr & Oct: to 4pm); adm ▪ Grounds: Nov–Mar: open 10am–4pm Fri–Sun; adm ▪ www.scone-palace.co.uk

Known as the "Fair City", Perth is situated on the tree-lined River Tay. Its streets are a delight of small shops for browsing. North of the city, off the A93, is Scone Palace. The grounds contain the Moot Hill, where Scottish kings were crowned on the famous Stone of Destiny *(see p12)*, now in Edinburgh Castle.

8 Discovery Point

MAP E5 ■ Dundee ■ (01382) 309 060 ■ Open Apr–Oct: 10am–6pm daily (from 11am Sun); Nov–Mar: 10am–5pm daily (from 11am Sun) ■ Adm ■ www.rrsdiscovery.com

The chill and hazards of Antarctic exploration grip you in this hi-tech exhibition. Focusing on the heroic and tragic expeditions of Shackleton and Scott, this display uses original film footage, modern images and inter-active computer screens. Tour the Dundee-built boat RSS *Discovery*, that carried Scott and his companions on their ill-fated expedition. While in Dundee visit the Contemporary Arts Centre on Nethergate for great exhibitions and its fine bistro-café.

9 Glamis Castle

MAP E5 ■ Glamis, Angus ■ (01307) 840 393 ■ Open Apr–Oct: 11am–5:30pm ■ Adm ■ www.glamis-castle.co.uk

A royal residence since 1372, this magical castle *(see p40)* with towers, turrets and treasures has a link with Shakespeare's *Macbeth*.

Interiors of the Glamis Castle

10 Pitlochry

MAP E4–5 ■ Theatre: (01796) 484 626 ■ Information Centre: 22 Atholl Rd; (01796) 472 215; open 9:30am–5:30pm Mon–Sat, 10am–4pm Sun (shorter hours in winter, longer in summer) ■ www.pitlochry.org

This tartan-and-tweed town has a long history of serving visitors. Its proximity to Perthshire's beauty spots and sporting estates was the original draw, but now it boasts a fine theatre and a fish ladder, where salmon leap up a series of pools to reach spawning grounds.

AN EAST COAST DRIVE

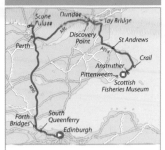

▶ MORNING

Leave Edinburgh around 9am and make for South Queensferry to photograph the iconic **Forth Bridges** *(see p94)*. There's an information centre where you can find out about the history of the bridges, and about the Queensferry Crossing.

Cross the road bridge and take the M90 to Perth. Stroll around the town, have a coffee, then follow the A93 to **Scone Palace** to see where Scottish kings such as Macbeth and Robert the Bruce were crowned. If you're hungry, have lunch here; they source ingredients from the palace kitchen garden.

Now it's about an hour's drive, via the A90 to Dundee where you can stop at **Discovery Point** and shiver at the exploits of the Antarctic explorers. Otherwise cross the Tay Bridge, then join the A919 to reach St Andrews, home to Scotland's oldest university and most famous golf course. There are plenty of places to eat.

AFTERNOON

You could easily spend the rest of the day strolling around St Andrews' quaint streets, but if you continue along the coast you'll come to the East Neuk fishing villages of Crail and Pittenweem *(see p91)* – not forgetting lovely Anstruther, where you'll find the **Scottish Fisheries Museum** *(see p94)*. Relax, soak up the scenery and enjoy a meal in one of the excellent fish restaurants *(see p95)*.

See map on p90

The Best of the Rest

① Hill of Tarvit Mansion

MAP F5 ■ Cupar ■ (01334) 653 127 ■ House: open Apr–Oct: 11am–4pm Sat–Tue (tours until noon) ■ Grounds: open 9am–dusk daily ■ Adm (free for NTS members) ■ www.nts.org.uk

This 17th-century mansion with vast grounds was remodelled in 1904 for a wealthy industrialist. It boasts cutting edge technology with electricity, telephones and central heating.

② Dunkeld

MAP E5

A village of great charm and character, with the noble ruins of its 14th-century cathedral and gorgeous riverside walks.

③ Kirriemuir and the Angus Glens

MAP E5

J M Barrie, creator of Peter Pan, was born in Kirriemuir; his birthplace is now a museum. Nearby are the wild and beautiful Angus Glens, great for scenic hikes.

Statue of Peter Pan, Kirriemuir

④ Loch Leven

MAP F5 ■ Adm

Mary, Queen of Scots, was imprisoned in this ruined castle. The loch provides a haven for birds – including ospreys.

⑤ Forth Bridges

MAP F5

The iconic cantilever rail bridge, suspension road bridge and the new Queensferry Crossing are best seen lit up at night.

⑥ Arbroath Abbey

MAP E6 ■ (01241) 878 756 ■ Open Apr–Sep: 9:30am–5:30pm daily; Oct–Mar: 10am–4pm daily ■ Adm (free for HES members)

The abbey makes for impressive ruins, but it's known for the copy of the "Declaration of Arbroath", Scotland's eloquent charter for independence.

⑦ Scottish Fisheries Museum

MAP F5 ■ Anstruther ■ (01333) 310 628 ■ Adm ■ www.scotfish museum.org

It's hard to believe just how fascinating boats, nets and fish can be. This museum offers a first-class overview of the history of the fish supper.

⑧ Verdant Works

MAP E5 ■ Dundee ■ (01382) 309 060 ■ Adm ■ www.verdantworks.com

Set in a refurbished mill, this is an invigorating presentation of the jute industry, the material upon which Dundee founded its urban economy.

⑨ Killiecrankie

MAP E4–5 ■ Pitlochry

The combined attractions here are a famous battle site and an idyllic river gorge. Admire the famous Soldier's Leap Queen Victoria loved this spot (and she was famously hard to please).

⑩ Montrose Basin Wildlife Centre

MAP E6 ■ (01674) 676 336 ■ Visitor Centre: open Mar–Oct: 10:30am–5pm daily (Nov–Feb: to 4pm Fri–Mon) ■ Adm ■ www.montrose basin.org.uk

Montrose is a tidal basin mecca for seafowl and waders. In winter, up to 80,000 pink-footed geese stop here during their migration.

Forth Rail Bridge from Queensferry Harbour

Places to Eat and Drink

1 Glen Clova Hotel
MAP E5 ■ Glen Clova, nr Kirriemuir ■ (01575) 550 350 ■ ££

Situated at the end of a lovely glen this hotel and restaurant has a simple all-day menu, which serves staples such as haddock, venison and steaks, as well as vegetarian options such as veggie haggis burgers.

2 Old Course Hotel
MAP F5 ■ St Andrews ■ (01334) 474 371 ■ £££

For lovers of traditional fine dining, the hotel's Road Hole Restaurant offers French-influenced cuisine, whereas the menu at Sands Grill is more cosmopolitan, journeying from North Africa to Italy.

3 63 Tay Street
MAP E5 ■ 63 Tay St, Perth ■ (01738) 441 451 ■ Closed D Sun & Mon ■ ££

This restaurant is the talk of the town, owing to chef Graeme Pallister. An extensive wine list complements a thrilling menu, which makes full use of Perthshire's prime natural larder.

4 Pillars of Hercules
MAP F5 ■ Strathmiglo Rd, Falkland ■ (01337) 857 749 ■ £

A family-friendly café, this place offers delicious vegetarian soups, sandwiches as well as main meals.

5 The Cellar
MAP F5 ■ Anstruther, Fife ■ (01333) 310 378 ■ £££

A seafood heaven, this restaurant (see p64) is set off a courtyard behind the Fisheries Museum. Enjoy meat dishes, and some of the best fish in Scotland. Some dishes feature garlic shoots and sea buckthorn.

Welcoming entrance of The Peat Inn

6 The Peat Inn
MAP F5 ■ Cupar ■ (01334) 840 206 ■ Closed Sun & Mon ■ £££

Experience exceptional food and range of wine at the fairest prices, at this popular restaurant (see p64).

7 Andrew Fairlie
MAP F4 ■ Gleneagles Hotel ■ (01764) 694 267 ■ Closed Sun ■ £££

French cuisine of high calibre is served amid a dreamy 1920s decor.

8 Jute Café Bar
MAP E5 ■ Dundee Contemporary Arts Centre, 152 Nethergate, Dundee ■ (01382) 909 246 ■ ££

The cavernous interior at the Jute Café Bar is ultrahip. There is a range of beers available and the menu offers imaginative dishes at extremely reasonable prices.

9 Ship Inn
MAP F5 ■ Elie, Fife ■ (01333) 330 246 ■ ££

Seasonal food is served in a converted boathouse overlooking the harbour of this village. There is a bar below, and a bistro on top. Vegetarian options are available.

10 The But 'n' Ben
MAP E6 ■ Auchmithie, nr Arbroath ■ (01241) 877 223 ■ ££

Within the white walls of this old fisherman's cottage, seafood is the speciality, especially Arbroath Smokies (see p65). You'll also find good venison and local produce here.

See map on p90

🔟 Glasgow

Stained-glass window, Glasgow Cathedral

Edinburgh may be the pretty sister, but Glasgow arguably has the more dynamic character, as exemplified by the outgoing and friendly Glaswegians. From the highs and lows of its storied past, the city of Glasgow has endured. Today it has reinvented itself as something of an epicentre of culture, cuisine, shopping and entertainment. Magnificent buildings are scattered across the city alongside first-rate restaurants, while the patronage of wealthy collectors has ensured the exceptional quality of Glasgow's many museums, art galleries and gardens.

GLASGOW

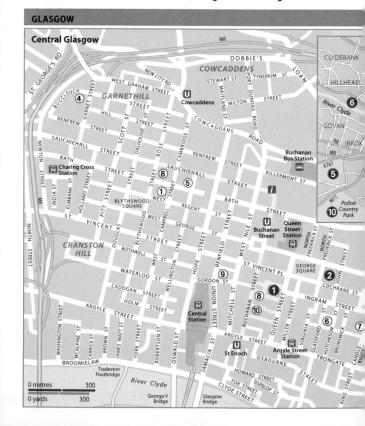

1 Gallery of Modern Art

MAP X4 ▪ Royal Exchange Square ▪ (0141) 287 3050 ▪ Open 10am–5pm daily (from 11am Fri–Sun; to 8pm Thu)

Glasgow's Gallery of Modern Art, or, more correctly, "of Astonishment", includes some works that immediately grab your attention, others that are deviously clever and a few that are outrageously funny. Exhibits change frequently, but the ethos remains essentially the same. Four main galleries feature painting, sculpture and modern photography in addition to permanent works by Scottish artists such as Peter Howson, Toby Paterson and John Byrne. In the basement is a sofa-adorned library, with a café and free internet access.

Lavish interior of City Chambers

2 City Chambers

MAP Y4 ▪ George Square ▪ (0141) 287 4018 ▪ By official tour only: open 10:30am & 2:30pm Mon–Fri ▪ www.glasgow.gov.uk

"Palace" would be a more appropriate term, for this is the finest seat of any council in Britain. Modelled on Classical Italian architecture, the building was designed by William Young and completed in 1889. The exterior is dramatic enough, but the interior is an exercise in the excesses of lavish decor. Aberdeen granite, Carrara marble, mahogany, gold leaf, frescoes, mosaics, pillars and balustrades are combined to astonishing effect. The Banqueting Hall – with its murals, chandeliers and ornately patterned ceiling and carpet – cannot fail to impress even the most jaded of visitors.

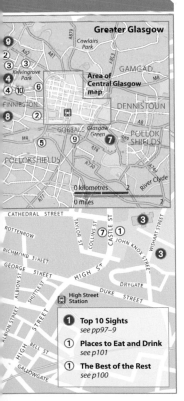

3 Glasgow Cathedral and Necropolis

MAP Z3 ▪ Cathedral Square ▪ (0141) 552 6891 ▪ Open 9:30am–5pm Mon–Sat, 1–4:30pm Sun (Oct–Mar: to 4pm)

Immense and ancient, this cathedral was ranked by Pope Nicholas V in 1451 as equal in merit to Rome as a place of pilgrimage. Dedicated in 1136 and completed almost a century later, it has been in continuous use since then and can boast original roof timbers. The choir screen is unique in Scotland, and the post-war stained-glass windows are exceptional. On a hill to the east looms the Necropolis, an extravagance of tombstones that is crowned by a monument to John Knox (see p14).

4 Kelvingrove Art Gallery and Museum

The most-visited collection *(see pp20–21)* in Scotland underwent a major refurbishment that doubled the museum's capacity, and provided the chance to display previously unseen works. Best of the bunch in Glasgow.

Stained glass, House for an Art Lover

5 House for an Art Lover

MAP Y3 ■ Bellahouston Park, Dumbreck Rd ■ (0141) 353 4770 ■ Open 10am–4pm Mon–Thu (times vary, so call ahead) ■ Adm ■ www.houseforanartlover.co.uk

In 1901 Glasgow's tour-de-force architect, Charles Rennie Mackintosh, and his artist wife, Margaret Macdonald, entered a magazine competition to design a "House for an Art Lover". It was to be "a grand house, thoroughly modern, fresh and innovative". Their exquisite vision remained just a design until 1989, when,

Exterior of Glasgow Science Centre

authentic to the smallest detail, the building and its contents were created. The café and shop are superb.

6 Riverside Museum

With acres of gleaming metalwork this museum *(see pp22–3)* has hundreds and hundreds of everything on wheels, including bicycles, cars, lorries, buses, trains and fire engines. You can walk through or climb into the larger vehicles, or sit in an original Glasgow tram. Upstairs are 250 model ships illustrating the story of Clyde shipbuilding. Watch out for the penny on the cobbles of the re-created 1938 shopping street – but don't try to pick it up, or you could be there all day. Make sure you also visit the Tall Ship, moored outside. Built in the 19th century, it has sailed around the world four times.

7 People's Palace

MAP Z3 ■ Glasgow Green ■ (0141) 276 0788 ■ Open 10am–5pm Tue–Sun (from 11am Fri & Sun) ■ www.glasgow museums.com

Typically Glaswegian, this is a museum of ordinary life. Nothing fancy or outstandingly old, but a fascinating insight into how the average family lived, worked and played in the not-so-distant past. There are prints, photos and films as well as an array of objects.

8 Glasgow Science Centre

Myriad puzzles, experiments and demonstrations *(see p61)* to entertain and inform. There's also an IMAX screen and a revolving tower – a sensational place.

Kibble Palace, Botanic Gardens

9 Botanic Gardens
MAP Z2 ▪ 730 Great Western
Rd, Glasgow ▪ (0141) 276 1614
▪ Gardens: open 7am–dusk daily
▪ Glasshouses: open 10am–6pm
daily (winter: to 4:15pm)

The highlights are the glasshouses
famous for their tropicana (see p49).

10 Burrell Collection and Pollok Park
MAP Y3 ▪ Pollokshaws Rd ▪ (0141)
616 6410 ▪ House: open 10am–5pm
▪ Adm (free for NTS members)
▪ www.nts.org.uk

Sir William Burrell's (1861–1958)
superb collection, housed in a
purpose-designed building in Pollok
Country Park, has long been one of
Glasgow's finest attractions. The
Burrell Collection will open in 2021
after refurbishment, and nearby Pollok
House is worth a visit. It gives a fascinating insight into Edwardian life and
boasts Spanish paintings by Murillo,
El Greco and Goya. There's a café in
the original kitchen, and lovely walks
in the surrounding wooded parkland.

ST MUNGO

A priest called St Mungo laid the
foundations of Glasgow when he
set up a monastery here in the 6th
century. A settlement grew up around
the monastery and prospered long
after the demise of that early religious
community. St Mungo's body lies
beneath the cathedral, and his
name has been given to a museum
(see p100) of religious art.

A FULL DAY IN GLASGOW

▶ MORNING

Take the subway to Kelvinhall
station (or walk from the city
centre) to visit **Kelvingrove Art
Gallery and Museum**. Allow a
couple of hours to explore and
don't miss the Dutch Old Masters
and French Impressionists.

Walk to the **Hunterian Art Gallery**
(see p100), on the other side of
Kelvingrove Park, to explore the
stunning House for an Art Lover,
a reassemblage of the interiors
of Charles Rennie Mackintosh's
home. Tours start at 10am (11am
on Sunday). Lunch at one of the
many cafés on the nearby Byres
Road or walk on to reach the
Botanic Gardens, where you can
picnic in the grounds or enjoy
a meal in their tearoom. Stroll
through the gardens and admire
the orchids in the enormous, tropical Kibble Palace glasshouse.

AFTERNOON

Take the subway to Cowcaddens
station, from where it's a short
walk to the **Tenement House**
(see p100). This intriguing, gas-lit
property is laid out much as it
was when it was home to Agnes
Toward in the early 20th century;
it's a real slice of old Glasgow life.

Hop back on the subway to
Buchanan Street station, where
you can choose to walk down to
elegant **Princes Square** (see p100)
to browse the shops, or make
your way across George Square
in time for the 2:30pm tour of
the City Chambers (see p97).
Have dinner at **City Merchant**
(see p101), one of the city's
many restaurants.

See map on pp96–7

The Best of the Rest

1 St Mungo Museum of Religious Art

MAP Z3 ▪ 2 Castle St ▪ (0141) 276 1625

Excellent overview of the world's religions through their art. The museum is illuminated by beautiful stained-glass windows.

2 Waverley Excursions

MAP Z3 ▪ Anderston Quay ▪ (0141) 243 2224 ▪ Open Jun–Aug ▪ www.waverleyexcursions.co.uk

Travel back in time and experience the Firth of Clyde on the world's last seagoing paddle steamer.

3 Hunterian Art Gallery

MAP Z2 ▪ 82 Hillhead St, nr Kelvingrove Park ▪ (0141) 330 4221 ▪ Open 10am–5pm Tue–Sat, 11am–4pm Sun ▪ Adm ▪ www.gla.ac.uk/hunterian

This gallery is best known for its collection of Rembrandts, its works by 19th-century American artist Whistler and the Mackintosh House.

4 Tenement House

MAP W2 ▪ 145 Buccleuch St ▪ (0141) 333 0183 ▪ Open Mar–Oct: 10am–5pm daily ▪ Adm

Tenements were standard Glasgow flats and Agnes Toward lived an ordinary life in this one, now a museum, for over 50 years.

5 Scotland Street School Museum

MAP Z3 ▪ 225 Scotland St ▪ (0141) 287 0500 ▪ Open 10am–5pm Tue–Thu & Sat (from 11am Fri & Sun)

Re-created Victorian, World War II and 1950s classrooms. Great fun.

6 Merchant City

MAP Y4

East of George Square is this grid-plan of streets where the "Tobacco Lords" built their warehouses and mansions. The area is now full of designer shops and restaurants.

7 Provand's Lordship

MAP Z3 ▪ 3 Castle St ▪ (0141) 276 1625 ▪ Open 10am–5pm Tue–Thu & Sat (from 11am Fri & Sun)

Built in 1471, this is the oldest house in Glasgow, with a fine furniture collection and cloistered herb garden.

8 Mackintosh at the Willow

MAP X3 ▪ 217 Sauchiehall St ▪ (0141) 332 7696 ▪ www.willowtearoomstrust.org

Designed by renowned Charles Rennie Mackintosh in 1903, this tea room is now an exhibition centre. After a tour, head for some tea and cake.

9 Citizens Theatre

MAP Z3 ▪ 119 Gorbals St ▪ (0141) 429 0022 ▪ www.citz.co.uk

An internationally famous venue; two modern studios complement the old Victorian auditorium.

10 Princes Square

MAP X4 ▪ 48 Buchanan St ▪ (0141) 221 0324

Luxurious shopping centre in a renovated square of 1841 – the genteel atmosphere found here is heightened by the occasional appearance of a piano player.

Princes Square shopping centre

Places to Eat and Drink

1 Brian Maule at Chardon D'Or
MAP X3 176 West Regent St (0141) 248 3801 Closed Sun £££

A true fine-dining experience that should not be missed (see p64). The chef, Brian Maule, combines the greatness of classic French cuisine with modern dishes that use top-quality Scottish produce.

2 Ubiquitous Chip
MAP Y2 12 Ashton Lane, off Byres Rd, Hillhead (0141) 334 5007 ££

Operating on this cobbled West End road since 1971, and always a champion of Scottish produce, the Ubiquitous Chip restaurant is Glasgow at its most endearing.

3 Stravaigin
MAP Z2 28 Gibson St, Hillhead (0141) 334 2665 ££

Where the nation's fish, beef, lamb and game are mixed with the world's sauces, herbs and spices. Eclectic mix of flavours, but Stravaigin's judicious touch wins the day.

4 Firebird
MAP Y2 1321 Argyle St, nr Riverside Museum (0141) 334 0594 ££

Firebird is a popular hangout for easy drinks and great pizzas – it's simple and consistently good.

5 Fratelli Sarti
MAP X3 121 Bath St & 133 Wellington St & 42 Renfield St (0141) 572 7000 ££

Lively Italian displaying a love of food in a living, breathing, everyday sense. Restaurant on Bath Street, with a café and deli around the corner.

6 Chinaski's
MAP Z2 239 North St (0141) 221 0061 £

The soundtrack here is one of the best in Glasgow, combining blues, soul and reggae. There is a heated deck and the food is enticing.

Vibrant exterior of the City Merchant

7 City Merchant
MAP Y4 97–99 Candleriggs (0141) 553 1577 ££

Looking like it's been around for aeons (though only in fact since the late 1980s), City Merchant is a Gallic-Scottish delight. Alongside some meaty mains, fish is the star.

8 Rogano
MAP X4 11 Exchange Place, off Exchange Square (0141) 248 4055 ££

A wonderful place to imbibe splendid cocktails in Art Deco surrounds. Pricey in the restaurant but fresh seafood is a bargain in the brasserie.

9 The Horseshoe Bar
MAP X4 17 Drury St (0141) 248 6368 £

Few pubs deserve to be considered a Glasgow institution more than this gem of a place. Friendly and cheap, it is a cracking pub in which to soak up the city's ambience.

10 Mother India
MAP Z2 28 Westminster Terrace, Sauchiehall St (0141) 221 1663 ££

A must-visit destination for gourmands of all stripes. You'll find exquisite modern Indian food here.

See map on pp96–7

TOP 10 North and West of Glasgow

This bucolic region became the focus of Scotland's first tourist industry in early Victorian times and, with Loch Lomond and the Trossachs National Park at its splendid centre, that allure remains as strong today. In the west are the rocky peaks of the Isle of Arran and a seaboard of fjord-like lochs, where a mild climate supports some grand gardens. In the east stands Stirling – a key city in the country's warring past – its mighty clifftop castle overlooking lush farmland. Here, William Wallace and Robert the Bruce fought for independence, a battle eventually won within sight of the castle on the field of Bannockburn.

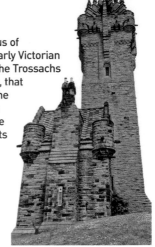

Wallace Monument

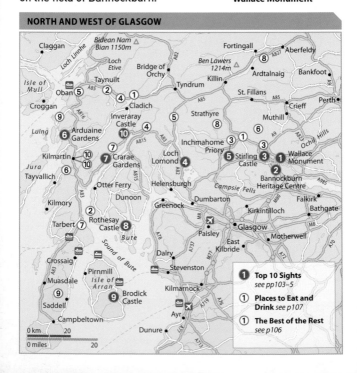

NORTH AND WEST OF GLASGOW

Claggan
Bidean Nam Bian 1150m △
Fortingall
Aberfeldy
Loch Linnhe
Loch Etive
Bridge of Orchy
Ben Lawers 1214m △
Ardtalnaig
Bankfoot
Taynuilt
Killin
St. Fillans
Isle of Mull
Oban ⑤ ② ④ ①
Tyndrum
Crieff
Perth
Croggan
⑨
Cladich
Strathyre
Muthill
Luing
Arduaine Gardens ⑥
Inveraray Castle ④
⑤
Inchmahome Priory ③ ①
⑥
Kilmartin ⑩ ⑩
⑦ ⑦ Crarae Gardens
Loch Lomond ④
Stirling Castle ⑤ ③ ③
Wallace Monument ①
Jura
Tayvallich ⑥
Otter Ferry
Helensburgh
Campsie Fells
Bannockburn Heritage Centre ②
Kilmory
②
Dunoon
Greenock
Dumbarton
Kirkintilloch
Falkirk
Bathgate
Tarbert ⑦
Rothesay Castle ⑧
Paisley
Glasgow
Motherwell
Bute
Sound of Bute
Dalry
East Kilbride
Crossaig
Stevenston
Muasdale
Pirnmill
Isle of Arran
Kilmarnock
Saddell
⑨
Brodick Castle ⑨
Ayr
Campbeltown
Dunure

0 km   20
0 miles   20

① **Top 10 Sights**
see pp103–5

① **Places to Eat and Drink** see p107

① **The Best of the Rest**
see p106

1 Wallace Monument

MAP F4 ▪ (01786) 472 140
▪ Open Apr–Jun, Sep & Oct: 9:30am–
5pm daily (Jul & Aug: to 6pm); Nov–Mar:
10:30am–4pm daily ▪ Adm ▪ www.
nationalwallacemonument.com

Erected in 1869, this 75-m (250-ft)
tower commemorates William
Wallace and his fight for Scotland's
independence. The climb takes you
past Wallace's two-handed broad-
sword. The electrifying "talking head"
presents Wallace's defence before
his brutal execution in 1305. There
are splendid 360° views from the top.

The scenic Trossachs National Park

2 Bannockburn Heritage Centre

MAP F4 ▪ Site: open all year
▪ Heritage Centre: open Apr–
late Sep: 9:30am–6pm daily;
Oct–late Mar: 10am–5pm
daily; adm (prebook, free for
NTS members); www.battle
ofbannockburn.com

The site of the decisive
battle (see p38) in 1314 is
marked by a visitor centre
and an equestrian statue
of Robert the Bruce. Kids
can try on helmets and
chain mail, and view Bruce's cave to
watch the fabled spider who inspired
him to renew his fight.

Robert the Bruce, Bannockburn

3 Stirling Castle

MAP F4 ▪ (01786) 450 000
▪ Open Apr–Sep: 9:30am–6pm daily
(Oct–Mar: to 5pm daily) ▪ Adm (free
for HES members)

Perched on a massive rock, the
Stirling Castle (see p40) conceals
the unique architecture of the restored
Great Hall and the Royal Palace.

4 Loch Lomond and the Trossachs National Park

MAP F4 ▪ www.lochlomond-
trossachs.org

The broad, friendly mountains
and poetic scenery of Scotland's
first national park are ideal
for the casual walker and
watersports lover. Luss is
the prettiest village in the
area. It hosts a popular
Highland Games (see p43)
in June and has good tea
shops. Cruises run from
here, and from Balloch,
Tarbet and Balmaha.

5 Inchmahome Priory

MAP F4 ▪ (01877) 385 294 ▪ Open
Apr–Oct: 10am–4:15pm (Oct: to
3:15pm) daily ▪ Adm ▪ www.historic
environment.scot

The Lake of Menteith is Scotland's
only lake (as opposed to loch), and
famed for the graceful ruined priory
on the island of Inchmahome. It's
in this beautiful spot that the infant
Mary Queen of Scots was looked
after by Augustinian monks before
she was spirited away to France.

Stirling Castle

6 Arduaine Gardens
MAP F3 ■ Nr Oban ■ (01852) 200 366 ■ Open 9:30am–sunset daily ■ Adm (free for NTS members)

A dazzling assembly of rhododendrons, azaleas, magnolias and hosts of exotic species from the Pacific Islands to the Himalayas. Arduaine *(see p49)* is beautifully situated on a promontory between sea lochs, and glories in the warm winds from the Gulf Stream.

7 Crarae Gardens
MAP F3 ■ Nr Inveraray ■ (01546) 886 614 ■ Open 9:30am–sunset daily; Visitor Centre: open Apr–Oct: 10am–5pm daily (Sep & Oct: Thu–Mon) ■ Adm (free for NTS members)

You don't have to be a rhododendron specialist to be bowled over by this beautifully manicured orchestration of colour *(see p49)*. An outstanding and rare collection, which is at its best in spring.

8 Rothesay Castle, Bute
MAP F3 ■ (01700) 502 691 ■ Open Apr–Sep: 9:30am–5:30pm daily; Oct–Mar: 10am–4pm Mon–Wed, Sat & Sun ■ Adm (free for HES members)

By virtue of its age, design and deep-water moat (one of only two remaining in Scotland), this is a remarkable medieval castle. Built

---

THE WONDERFUL WORLD OF CRARAE GARDENS

Lady Grace Campbell began to lay out the gardens in 1912, making exciting use of plant specimens that her nephew Reginald Farrer brought back from his travels to Tibet and the Himalayas. On the higher ground is the forest-garden, a feature that is found nowhere else in Britain, where more than 100 tree species grow under forest conditions on their own plots. Crarae is considered of international importance and is a member of "Glorious Gardens of Argyll and Bute" (*www.gardens-of-argyll.co.uk*).

Rothesay Castle, Bute

around 1200s as a defence against Norwegian raiders, it was restyled in the 13th century and fitted with high curtain walls and drum towers. Its circular courtyard is a curious feature and unique in Scotland. Bute itself is a mere 35-minute crossing from Wemyss Bay – north of Largs on the A78 – to Rothesay Bay; an even shorter crossing is from Colintraive to Rhubodach, on the north coast of the island.

9 Brodick Castle, Arran
MAP G3 ■ (01770) 302 202 ■ Castle, Tearoom and Park: open Apr–Oct: 10am–5pm daily ■ Adm (free for NTS members) ■ www.nts.org.uk

Originally a Viking keep before the Dukes of Hamilton claimed it, this 13th-century fortified tower was extended by Oliver Cromwell and then transformed into a stately home in Victorian times. The last Hamilton moved out only in 1957. A solid red sandstone building with fanciful trimmings, it contains a noted collection of silver, porcelain and paintings. The gardens are beautifully maintained (try to catch the rhododendrons in spring bloom), as are the woodland trails. The main ferry to Arran (just under an hour) is from Ardrossan, on the mainland coast, just north of Irvine.

10 Inveraray Castle

MAP F3 ■ (01499) 302 203
■ Open Apr–Oct: 10am–5:45pm daily
■ Adm ■ www.inveraray-castle.com

Despite the ravages of fire, Clan Campbell's (see p43) family seat is a splendid pseudo-Gothic palace with pointed towers. It was built for the Duke of Argyll in 1745. The interiors were designed by Robert Mylne and contain Regency furniture and price-less works of art. The Armoury Hall was stocked to fight the Jacobites. There's a hilltop folly in the grounds. The castle grounds host the Inveraray Highland Games, a colourful celebra-tion of Highland culture.

Armoury Hall, Inveraray Castle

A DAY IN THE TROSSACHS

▶ MORNING

Reserve your morning cruise on the *SS Sir Walter Scott* ((01877) 376 315, call in advance; www.loch katrine.com).

Leaving Glasgow by 8.15am, drive north on the A81 to **Strathblane** and **Aberfoyle**. You are now in the scenic **Trossachs** (see p103). Park at the **Trossachs Pier** for a 10:30am cruise on **Loch Katrine** (see p44), a gorgeous loch.

Arriving back at 12:30pm, a short drive takes you to Kilmahog (great name, but the Woollen Mill is worth visit if you're curious about knitwear). Head on to Callander, where you can stop for lunch at one of several restaurants, or buy delicious pies at the **Mhor Bread & Tearoom** (Map F4; 8 Main St, Callander; (01877) 339 518; closed D) and picnic by the river.

AFTERNOON

Carry on to **Doune, Dunblane and Bridge of Allan**. There are many temptations en route, including the **Doune Castle** (see p106), a cathedral and a motor museum.

If not, head to **Wallace Monument** (see p103) before 4pm, and earlier in winter. Enjoy the history and the panoramic views of the area, including the craggy heights of **Stirling Castle** (see p103).

Head back to Glasgow for an early dinner in the city centre (see p101). For those who can wait, Edinburgh or **St Andrews** (see p92) are only slightly further towards the east (each about an hour's drive).

See map on p102 ←

The Best of the Rest

The majestic Kilchurn Castle

1 Kilchurn Castle
MAP E3 ■ Open Apr–late Sep: 9:30am–5:30pm daily

The hauntingly atmospheric ruins of the Campbell castle, built in 1440 on an island to the northeast of Loch Awe, are visible from many points.

2 Bonawe Historic Iron Furnace
MAP E3 ■ Taynuilt ■ (01866) 822 432 ■ Open Apr–Sep: 9:30am–5:30pm Wed–Fri ■ Adm (free for HES members) ■ www.historic-scotland.gov.uk

Set by Loch Etive are the best-preserved charcoal-fuelled ironworks. Learn how iron was made in 1753.

3 Doune Castle
MAP F4 ■ (01786) 841 742 ■ Open Apr–Sep: 9:30am–5:30pm daily; Oct–Mar: 10am–4pm daily ■ Adm

This 14th-century castle has a magical air about it. Perhaps most enchanting is the Lord's Hall, with its musicians' gallery and double fireplace.

4 Cruachan Hollow Mountain Power Station
MAP E3 ■ Nr Lochawe ■ (0141) 614 9105 ■ Open Apr–Oct: 9:15am–4:45pm daily (Nov, Dec, Feb & Mar: to 3:45pm Mon–Fri) ■ Adm ■ www.visitcruachan.co.uk

Tunnels and underground caverns make this massive hydroelectric plant seem like a science-fiction set.

5 Oban
MAP E3 ■ Visitor Info: (01631) 563 122

This busy harbour town is best seen from McCaig's Folly. There are many local attractions here and ferries travelling to Mull, Coll, Colonsay, Tiree and the Western Isles.

6 Crinan Canal
MAP F3

Take a stroll along this scenic 16-km (9-mile) canal, completed in 1801, and now used by yachts and fishing boats. The best places to see them are at Ardrishaig, Cairnbaan or Crinan.

7 Auchindrain Township
MAP F3 ■ Nr Inveraray ■ (01499) 500 235 ■ Open Apr–Oct: 10am–5pm daily (Nov–Mar: to 4pm Sat & Sun; call ahead to check open times) ■ Adm ■ www.auchindrain.org.uk

A novel outdoor museum of restored thatched cottages and outbuildings, Auchindrain displays the past styles of West Highland life.

8 Scottish Crannog Centre
MAP E4 ■ Kenmore ■ (01887) 830 583 ■ Open Apr–Oct: 10am–5:30pm daily ■ Adm ■ www.crannog.co.uk

The little-known and ancient art of building crannogs (defensive home-steads built on stilts in lochs) has been rediscovered here at Loch Tay.

9 Kintyre
MAP G3 ■ www.kintyre.org

Paul McCartney sang about this glorious peninsula, which has miles of beaches, a top golf course (Machrihanish) and the ethereal cave crucifixion painting on Davaar Island.

10 Kilmartin Glen
MAP F3

Inhabited for 5,000 years, Kilmartin Glen has a concentration of archae-ological remains: standing stones, temples and burial cairns. Pause at Kilmartin Church for the best collection of early Christian crosses.

Places to Eat and Drink

1 The Roman Camp
MAP F4 ■ Callander
■ (01877) 330 003 ■ £££

Voluptuous curtains, deep sofas and blazing fires make this country hotel a delight, and the restaurant excels. Their Sunday lunch special, rump of lamb, is a winner.

2 Marina Restaurant
MAP F3 ■ Portavadie, Loch Fyne ■ (01700) 811 075 ■ ££

Fresh seafood and Loch Fyne oysters are served in this lovely restaurant that boasts splendid views of Kintyre and the distant Arran Hills.

3 Lake Of Menteith
MAP F4 ■ Port of Menteith
■ (01877) 385 258 ■ ££

Housed in a lovely conservatory, this smart lakeside restaurant's menu serves well-executed Scottish fare.

Loch Fyne Oyster Bar

4 Loch Fyne Oyster Bar
MAP F3 ■ Cairndow, nr Inveraray ■ (01499) 600 482 ■ ££

Long established in this converted stone cattle byre, the oyster bar offers two vegetarian dishes daily and an ocean of the freshest seafood. Bring a hearty appetite and have a go at the lobster platter.

5 The Drover's Inn
MAP F4 ■ Inverarnan, Loch Lomond ■ (01301) 704 234 ■ ££

A flagstone floor, cobwebbed walls and a menagerie of stuffed animals to fight your way past – it's quite an experience. Good ol' pub grub and amber fluid flow all day.

6 The Kailyard
MAP F4 ■ Perth Rd, Dunblane FK15 0HG ■ (01786) 822 551 ■ ££

Fine Scottish produce is served at this hotel restaurant, run by celebrity chef Nick Nairn. The dishes served include Scotch beef and Scrabster sole. It also has a good vegetarian menu.

7 Starfish
MAP F2 ■ Castle St, Tarbert
■ (01880) 820 733 ■ ££

Set in a picturesque fishing village, this friendly and relaxed restaurant with local art on the walls serves up langoustines, lobster, scallops, crab and other seafood – all of which is landed daily at the nearby quay.

8 The Waterfront
MAP E4 ■ Kenmore
■ (01877) 830 555 ■ ££

Overlooking Loch Tay, this sleek and modern restaurant serves dishes prepared with fresh local produce. Try the haddock, venison and sea trout. Vegetarian options are available.

9 Tigh-an-Truish
MAP F3 ■ Clachan, Isle of Seil
■ (01852) 300 242 ■ ££

Old-world inn by the famous "Bridge over the Atlantic"; you half expect pirates to breeze in. Real ale and delicious local food.

10 Kilmartin Museum Café
MAP F3 ■ Kilmartin ■ (01546) 510 278 ■ £

An adjunct of the Kilmartin Museum, this light-lunch café is mainly vegetarian, but serves excellent venison burgers as well.

See map on p102

🔟 Grampian and Moray

The northeastern corner of Scotland, a veritable medley of landscapes, is home to equally diverse industries, from the traditions of farming, fishing and distilling to the more recent business of North Sea oil extraction. The high granite massif of the Cairngorms is primed for mountain sports. Then comes the forested splendour of Royal Deeside, Queen Victoria's beloved retreat, and the quilted fields of Buchan's rich farmland. Along the River Spey is the heartland of whisky production, while on the coast are beaches, cliffs and enchanting fishing villages.

Bishop Elphinstones tomb at Old Aberdeen

1 Aberdeen

MAP D6 ▪ Aberdeen Science Centre: 179 Constitution St; (01224) 640 340 ▪ Provost Skene's House, Guestrow: (01224) 641 086 ▪ Maritime Museum, Shiprow: (01224) 337 700 ▪ Art Gallery, Schoolhill: (03000) 200 293; closed for refurbishment

The "Granite City" has beautiful buildings, year-round floral displays and a beach fringed with entertainment, including the Beach Leisure Centre (see p61) and the Aberdeen Science Centre, a science discovery complex. Provost Skene's House (once home to a 17th-century *provost*, or mayor, of Aberdeen) is the oldest building, dating from 1545, while Marischal College is one of the world's largest granite edifices. The Maritime Museum charts the nautical world from shipbuilding to shipwrecks. The Art Gallery, closed for refurbishment, mixes temporary contemporary shows with a permanent collection spanning the 19th–20th centuries.

GRAMPIAN AND MORAY

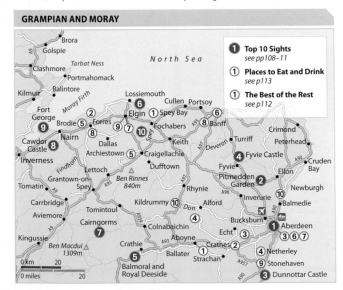

Top 10 Sights
see pp108–11

Places to Eat and Drink
see p113

The Best of the Rest
see p112

The meticulously landscaped Great Garden, Pitmedden Garden

2 Pitmedden Garden
MAP D6 ■ Ellon ■ (01651) 842 352 ■ Grounds: daily ■ Garden, museum & shop: open Apr–late Sep: 10:30am–4:30pm daily (Oct: Fri–Mon) ■ Adm (free for NTS members)

The striking symmetry of the formal Great Garden *(see p49)* is unique. Here are idyllic pond and wildlife gardens, and a Museum of Farming Life.

3 Dunnottar Castle
MAP E6 ■ Nr Stonehaven ■ (01569) 766 320 ■ Open Apr–Sep: 9am–5:30pm daily; Oct–Mar: 10am–4:30pm daily ■ Adm ■ www. dunnottarcastle.co.uk

Few castles match Dunnottar's setting. Standing heroically isolated on a rock, only few castles have endured such intense bombardments. In 1651, while harbouring the Scottish regalia, secretly smuggled out by a brave woman, it withstood an eight-month siege by the English. Its dungeons, have seen sufferings and deaths. Some 800 years of attack have taken their toll, but Dunnottar remains a mythical sight.

4 Fyvie Castle
MAP D6 ■ Nr Turriff ■ (01651) 891 266 ■ Castle: open Apr–May: 11am–4pm daily (Jun & Sep: to 4:30pm; Oct–mid-Dec: to 3pm Fri–Mon); guided tours only ■ Garden: 9am–sunset daily ■ Adm ■ www.nts.org.uk

Dating from 1390, this formidable building, which once hosted Charles I, is one of the finest examples of Scottish Baronial architecture. Its life through the ages is testified to by the mix of contemporary panelling, 17th-century plaster work and treasure trove of collectable paintings, arms and armour. The restored 19th-century Victorian walled garden specializes in Scottish fruit and vegetables.

Fyvie Castle

Balmoral Castle, the Queen's summer residence in Royal Deeside

5 Balmoral and Royal Deeside

MAP D5 ▪ (01339) 742 534 ▪ Open Apr–Jul: 10am–5pm daily ▪ Adm ▪ www.balmoralcastle.com

Queen Victoria bought this castle – her "dear paradise" – in 1852. Balmoral, bordering the salmon pools of the River Dee, remains the holiday home of the monarch to this day and, consequently, the rolling countryside around the banks of the river has taken on the royal moniker. Cast an eye round the castle's sumptuous ballroom, then make the most of the enchanting forest walks.

6 Moray Coast Villages

MAP C5–6

These charming communities thrived in the herring boom of the 19th century, but today only Lossiemouth,

Buckie (with its excellent Drifter Museum), Macduff and Fraserburgh continue as fishing ports. For many visitors, Crovie (pronounced "crivie") is the pick of the bunch. Access from the car park is by foot only, its picturesque street strung out below the cliffs – it truly is a fabulous setting. The walk to Gardenstown is an adventure for the sure-footed. Findhorn – famous for its spiritual community – is beautifully located on a sandy lagoon. A self-drive tour of the coastal road (highly recommended) will reveal a dozen other villages, each one possessing its own unique character.

Crovie village, Moray Coast

VICTORIA AND ALBERT'S BALMORAL

It was the riverside setting that Victoria fell for in 1848 when she first visited Balmoral. And it was her husband Albert who worked with the Aberdeen-born architect William Smith to create the white granite palace that replaced the old castle and stands here still, a medley of fantastical turrets typical of the Baronial style.

7 Cairngorms

A superb range of mountain peaks *(see pp34–5)* surrounded by pine forests and lochs. Ideal for testing walks, lively watersports and inspiring scenery.

8 Cawdor Castle

MAP D4 ■ Nr Nairn ■ (01667) 404 401 ■ Open May–early Oct: 10am–5:30pm daily ■ Adm ■ www.cawdor castle.com

A private home, handed down through the generations since the time when Macbeth lived here (or so legend has it). Cawdor Castle *(see p41)* is full of history and delight, with creepy relics, magnificent trees and a garden maze.

9 Fort George

MAP D4

On a peninsula jutting into the Moray Firth is this vast fort complex *(see p29)*, built at enormous expense 250 years ago and still used as an army barracks today. Impressive defences now guard a vintage armoury. Check out the special summer events.

10 The Whisky Trail

Seven of Scotland's finest malt whisky distilleries *(see p35)* invite you inside. Apart from the magic of the shining copper stills, the once-secretive process of whisky-making is revealed, enthusiasm infused and the precious *uisge beatha* (water of life) consumed.

A DAY'S DRIVING TOUR

▶ MORNING

Leave **Aberdeen** *(see p108)* around 9am and drive on the A93 through Deeside's splendid scenery to Crathie, where you'll find the castle in **Balmoral** opening its gates. If, however, you're outside Balmoral's short opening season, then visit **Crathes Castle** or **Drum Castle** *(see p112)* instead – less famous, but equally impressive.

Return to Ballater, the nearest town to Balmoral Castle which you passed through on the way, but this time take the B976 on the south of the river. There are plenty of places to eat, offering anything from a bacon sandwich or pain au chocolat to a three-course meal.

AFTERNOON

While browsing the shops in Ballater, look out for royal insignias: they indicate the Queen's favourite establishments.

From Ballater find the A939 and drive north on a twisting road. The terrain is wild, heathery moorland and mountainous. The road takes you past quaint and lonely Corgarff Castle, and on to Tomintoul, one of the highest villages in Scotland. From here, take the B9008 to the distillery of **Glenlivet** *(see p60)* for a tour of their whisky-making vats, stills and barrels, and a tasting. Tours last about 75 minutes; the tastings, unfortunately, much less.

Spend the night around Dufftown or Keith and plan to drive to Portsoy on the coast road either east or west the next day. The tour is about 150 km (90 miles) in total.

See map on p108 ←

The Best of the Rest

1 Moray Firth Dolphins
MAP D4 ■ Info Centre: (01343) 820 339 ■ Boat trips from Inverness: (07544) 800 620; from Cromarty: (01381) 600 323

The only known resident population of bottlenose dolphins in the North Sea.

2 Crathes Castle
MAP D6 ■ Banchory ■ (01330) 844 525 ■ Castle: open Apr–Oct: 10:30am–5pm daily; Nov–Mar: 11am–4pm Sat & Sun ■ Grounds: open all year ■ Adm (free for NTS members)

A 16th-century tower house, with a traditional Great Hall. There are topiary and plant sales Easter to October.

3 Drum Castle
MAP D6 ■ Nr Banchory ■ (01330) 700 334 ■ Castle: open Apr, May, Sep & Oct: 10:30am–4pm Thu–Mon (Jul & Aug: daily); Nov & Dec: Sat & Sun) ■ Grounds: open all year ■ Adm (free for NTS members)

This is one of the three oldest surviving tower houses in Scotland.

4 Craigievar Castle
MAP D6 ■ (01339) 883635 ■ Castle: open Apr & May: 10:30am–4pm Fri–Tue (Jun–Sep: daily; Oct: to 3pm Sat & Sun) ■ Grounds: open all year ■ Adm (free for NTS members)

A tower house with porcelain details. There are monkey puzzle trees here.

Craigievar Castle in a lush setting

5 Brodie Castle
MAP D4 ■ Forres, nr Nairn ■ (01309) 641 371 ■ Castle: open Mar–Jun & Sep–Oct 10am–5pm daily (Nov–Feb: to 4pm); Jul–Aug 9:30am–6pm daily ■ Grounds: open all year ■ Adm (free for NTS members)

This Z-Plan tower house has survived many attacks and contains a treasury of furniture and paintings.

6 Duff House Gallery
MAP C6 ■ Banff ■ (01261) 818 181 ■ Open Apr–Sep: 9:30am–5:30pm daily; Oct–Mar: 10am–4pm Fri–Sun ■ Adm (free for HES members) ■ www.historicenvironment.scot

The collection at this Georgian mansion includes works by Ramsay and Raeburn, as well as El Greco.

7 Elgin Cathedral
MAP C5 ■ (01343) 547 171 ■ Open Apr–Sep: 9:30am–5:30pm daily; Oct–Mar: 10am–4pm daily ■ Adm (free for HES members)

Burned out of spite by the Wolf of Badenoch in 1390, this cathedral's picturesque ruins draw a crowd.

8 Dallas Dhu Distillery
MAP C5 ■ Forres, nr Nairn ■ (01309) 676548 ■ Open Apr–Sep: 9:30am–5:30pm daily; Oct–Mar: 10am–4pm Sat–Wed (last entry 30 mins before closing) ■ Adm (free for HES members)

When this working distillery closed, it was preserved as a time capsule of whisky-making from 1898 to 1980.

9 Stonehaven
MAP E6

Close to Dunnottar Castle (see p109), this seaside resort has an open-air Olympic-size swimming pool.

10 Kildrummy Castle
MAP D5 ■ Nr Alford ■ (01975) 571 1331 ■ Open Apr–Sep: daily ■ Adm (free for HES members)

The once "noblest of northern castles" is now a grandiose ruin. It retains many unique 13th-century features.

Places to Eat and Drink

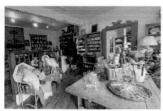

At the Sign of the Black Faced Sheep

PRICE CATEGORIES
For a three-course meal for one with half a bottle of wine (or equivalent meal), taxes and extra charges.

£ under £30 ££ £30–60 £££ over £60

1 At the Sign of the Black Faced Sheep

MAP D5 ■ Ballater Rd, Aboyne ■ (01339) 887 311 ■ £

Emporium with an upmarket coffee shop serving interesting sandwiches, sun-dried tomato scones, seafood platters, daily specials and great cakes.

2 The Bakehouse Cafe

MAP C5 ■ 91-92 Findhorn Rd, Forres ■ (01309) 691826 ■ £

This is a great place for vegetarian dishes and organic produce. It does some delicious home baking as well.

3 210 Bistro

MAP D6 ■ 210 South Market St, Aberdeen ■ (01224) 211857 ■ Closed Sun ■ ££

The downstairs café and bar forms a relaxing anteroom between bustling Market Street and the upstairs restaurant with its minimalist decor, and harbour views. The menu features fresh and beautifully presented Scottish dishes.

4 Crynoch Restaurant

MAP E6 ■ Lairhillock Inn, Netherley, Stonehaven ■ (01569) 730 001 ■ www.lairhillock.co.uk ■ ££

Rustic decor and family atmosphere delivering modern cuisine with flair. Specialities such as king prawns in lime, chilli and coconut sauce or roast chicken stuffed with artichoke mousse grace the menu.

5 Archiestown Hotel

MAP D5 ■ The Square, Archiestown, nr Craigellachie ■ (01340) 810 218 ■ Closed 3 Jan–9 Feb & 23–28 Dec ■ ££

Popular with fishermen, the bistro here has earned a good reputation. Wild salmon is a regular speciality.

6 The Silver Darling

MAP D6 ■ Pocra Quay, Aberdeen ■ (01224) 576 229 ■ ££

One of the best restaurants in the country, this seafood emporium *(see p65)* overlooks the Aberdeen harbour.

A dish at Moonfish Café

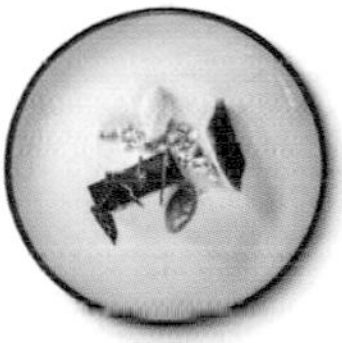

7 Moonfish Café

MAP D6 ■ 9 Correction Wynd, Aberdeen ■ (01224) 644 166 ■ ££

Tucked away in a lane, this place is known for some of Aberdeen's most inventive fare.

8 The Seafield Arms

MAP D5–6 ■ Whitehills, nr Banff ■ (01261) 861 209 ■ ££

Set on the Moray Firth, this inn focuses on seafood dishes. Try the baked haddock with tiger prawns.

9 The Sunninghill Hotel

MAP C5 ■ Hay St, Elgin ■ (01343) 547 799 ■ ££

Popular with locals, this hotel serves traditional Scottish dishes such as steak pie and fresh haddock with chips.

10 Cock and Bull

MAP D6 ■ Ellon Rd, Balmedie ■ (01358) 743 249 ■ ££

Rustic meets trendy in this blend of country inn and contemporary gastro-pub. Try the fish cakes or a juicy burger.

See map on p108

TOP 10 The Highlands

The name alone evokes thoughts of mountains, heather, bagpipes, castles, clans, romance and tragedy – indeed, the Highlands have it all. It is the combination of peerless scenery, enduring traditions and nostalgia (albeit for a rather idealized past) that gives the Highlands their irresistible allure. The weather is not always great, but rain brings out the best in waterfalls. It's a sparsely inhabited region, where you may still find single-track roads and more sheep than people. Life takes on a slower pace, and often hotels and restaurants work shorter hours, but the great compensation is peace. Little wonder that so many aspects of the Highlands have been adopted as symbols of the nation as a whole.

Memorial Cairn, Culloden Battlefield

THE HIGHLANDS

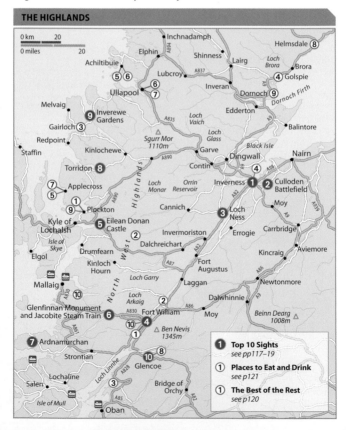

1 Top 10 Sights
see pp117–19

1 Places to Eat and Drink
see p121

1 The Best of the Rest
see p120

Previous pages Dunnottar Castle, Aberdeenshire

Majestic Castle Wynd, Inverness

1 Inverness

MAP D4 ■ Tourist Info: (01463) 252 401 ■ Museum & Gallery: Castle Wynd; open Tue–Sat; adm ■ Viewpoint: open Apr, May, Sep & Oct: 11am–6pm daily; Jun: 10am–7pm daily; Jul & Aug 9am–8pm daily; Nov–Mar: 11:30am–4pm Fri–Mon; adm ■ Abertarff House: open 11am–6pm daily in summer, shorter hours in winter

A fast-growing city with a small-town feel, Inverness is redeemed from the blight of its dull modern architecture by the majestic red sandstone castle (which boasts a viewing platform in the tower), fine old houses and the beauty of the River Ness. Inverness Museum and Art Gallery invites "hands on the Highland Heritage" (but you have to leave the artifacts behind), and Abertarff House. The Islands Walk is sublimely peaceful.

2 Culloden Battlefield

MAP D4 ■ Visitor Centre: (01463) 796 090; open Nov–Feb: 10am–4pm daily, Mar–May, Sept & Oct: 9am–6pm daily (Jun–Aug: to 7pm) ■ Adm (free for NTS members) ■ www.nts.org.uk

The last battle on British soil, 16th April 1746, was a defeat for Bonnie Prince Charlie and the Jacobites (see p38). The slaughter by the "Bloody Butcher's" (the Duke of Cumberland's) Hanoverian army was quick and brutal. The battlefield is gradually being restored to its appearance at the time of the bloodshed. To walk among the graves of the clans is still a peculiarly emotional experience. The Memorial Cairn, which was erected here in 1881, stands 6 m (20 ft) high. The story is well illustrated in the visitor centre.

3 Loch Ness

Ice Age glaciers gouged out a deep trench along a split in the land mass of Scotland, and the resulting valley is known as the Great Glen. Loch Ness (see pp28–9) is its cause célèbre, with arresting views, the mystery of its reclusive monster and the evocative ruins of Urquhart Castle.

4 Ben Nevis and Fort William

MAP E3 ■ Tourist Info: (01397) 701 801 ■ West Highland Museum: (01397) 702 169; open Mon–Sat (Jul & Aug: Sun) ■ Treasures of the Earth: (01397) 772 283; open year-round

Britain's highest mountain (see p46) is 1,345 m (4,411 ft) high and offers a great walk in good conditions. But the peak is frequently shrouded in mist, and the drive up Glen Nevis offers a more reliable reward, taking you to a waterfall. Fort William (see p20) a major shopping town lies below the mountain, with plenty of attractions. Its West Highland Museum has many Jacobite relics, and Treasures of the Earth exhibits glittering heaps of gems.

Ben Nevis behind Fort William

5 Eilean Donan Castle

MAP D3 ■ Visitor centre: (01599) 555 202 ■ Open Feb–Dec: 10am–4pm daily (Mar–Oct: to 6pm) ■ Adm ■ www.eileandonancastle.com

Restored in 13th-century, this majestic fortress *(see p41)* of Clan Macrae stands on a picturesque island on the road to Skye.

6 Glenfinnan Monument and Jacobite Steam Train

MAP E3 ■ Visitor centre: (01397) 722 250; open Apr–Sep: 9am–7pm daily; Mar & Oct: 9:30am–5pm; Nov–Feb 10am–4pm; adm (free for NTS members ■ Jacobite Steam Train: (01524) 732 100; open May–Oct

This is another memorial to the Jacobite uprising led by Bonnie Prince Charlie *(see p38)*, on the site where his campaign began. Here, a visitor centre explains the history. The chief attraction is getting here – the scenery en route is stunning. Take time to marvel at the nearby viaduct (featured in the Harry Potter films) and wait for a passing steam train – or even better, be in a passing steam train.

Camas nan Geall, Ardnamurchan

Glenfinnan Monument

RETURN OF THE BONNIE PRINCE

Set on reclaiming the British Crown for the Stuart line, Bonnie Prince Charlie landed on the west coast of Scotland in 1745 with but a handful of men. His temerity, as well as widespread support for the Jacobite cause, won over many Scots, and when he came to raise his standard at Glenfinnan, numbers swelled as clans such as the Camerons rallied to his side.

7 Ardnamurchan

MAP E2 ■ Natural History Centre: (01972) 500 209; open Apr–Oct: 8:30am–5pm daily; www.ardnamurchan naturalhistorycentre.co.uk

This peninsula – with its rugged mountains, pretty villages and what is one of the most delightful roads in the country, ending in a parade of white sand – is as lyrical in nature as it is in name. Acharacle is a famed den of musicians, while Glenmore is home to a Natural History Centre with a tearoom, gift shop and a "living building". Wild deer sometimes graze on its roof. From Kilchoan you can catch a ferry to Tobermory on Mull.

Torridon Hills, near Torridon village

8 Torridon

MAP D3 ▪ Countryside Centre: (01445) 791 221; open Apr–Sep: 10am–5pm Sun–Fri ▪ www.nts.org.uk

Flanked by a long sea loch, the red sandstone buttresses of Beinn Alligin, Ben Dearg, Liathach (the highest, see p47) and Beinn Eighe rise up into arresting outlines. From Little Diabaig you can walk a delightful coastal path to Alligin Shuas, or to Craig. The National Trust for Scotland runs an informative Countryside Centre with nearby herds of red deer and Highland cattle.

9 Inverewe Gardens

MAP C3 ▪ Nr Poolewe ▪ (01445) 781 229/ 712 952 ▪ Open Jan–late May & Sep: 9:30am–5pm daily (Jun–late Aug: to 6pm; Oct: to 4pm) ▪ Adm (free for NTS members)

Butterfly, Inverewe Gardens

The sheer richness and variety of plant life growing here (see p49) in what many consider to be a cold wilderness is a tribute to a plant enthusiast's vision and hard work, nature's bounty and the surprising benign effects of warm Atlantic winds.

10 Glencoe

A rugged mountain range (see pp30–31) gathered into gorgeous scenery through which the twisting main road seems to creep submissively. A favourite skiing, mountaineering and walking area, and infamous for the terrible 1692 massacre of Clan MacDonald (see p30).

A HIGHLAND DAY TRIP

▶ MORNING

Pack a picnic in Inverness (see p117). There are lots of picnicking possibilities on this route, so make sure to take one.

Leave Inverness by 10am, taking the B852 to Dores and driving along the south side of Loch Ness (see p117) – a beautiful and much quieter road than that on the northern shore. Try to stop off at the Falls of Foyers (see p58).

Enjoy the hill-country drive to Fort Augustus (see p29), and pop in for a coffee at The Lock Inn (Map D4; Canal Side, PH32 4AU; (01320) 366 302), right beside the canal. Walk along the canal to view Loch Ness from the shore behind the old abbey.

Drive along the A82 on the north side of Loch Ness (stop at Invermoriston to view the river pools and old bridge) and visit Urquhart Castle (see p29). Have your picnic lunch here.

AFTERNOON

Having recharged your batteries sufficiently, visit one of the Loch Ness Monster Visitor Centres (see p29) in Drumnadrochit.

Refill your thermos in Drumnadrochit, then take the A831 to Cannich, and the minor road to Glen Affric (see p120).

Enjoy an hour's walk in this renowned beauty spot, before returning to the bustle of Inverness via Kilmorack and the south shore of the Beauly Firth. The entire round trip is about 185 km (115 miles).

See map on p116

The Best of the Rest

Pretty village of Plockton

1 Plockton
MAP D3

Prime candidate for the title of Scotland's prettiest west coast village, Plockton has sea, palm trees and a Rare Breeds Farm.

2 Glen Affric
MAP D3

Glen Affric (see p28) is an example of nature's outstanding beauty, most easily accessed from the east at Cannich. At the western end, near Morvich, there's a walk to the breathtaking Falls of Glomach.

3 Gairloch Heritage Museum
MAP C3 ▪ Gairloch ▪ (01445) 712 287 ▪ Open daily ▪ Adm ▪ www.gairloch heritagemuseum.org

A leader of its kind, this redeveloped exhibition excels with a programme of old-industry demonstrations, such as spinning, corn-milling and butter-churning. Exhibits include a Pictish stone, a 1940s shop as well as a 'midgeater' that was created to repel the insect, Highland midge.

4 Dunrobin Castle
MAP C4 ▪ Golspie ▪ (01408) 633 177 ▪ Open Apr–mid-Oct ▪ Adm

A home befitting its wealthy landowners, the dukes of Sutherland. Towers, turrets and a palatial interior upon which no expense has been spared. Garden falconry displays too.

5 The Hydroponicum, Achiltibuie
MAP C3 ▪ (01854) 622 202 ▪ Call ahead to book a visit ▪ Adm ▪ www.thehydroponicum.com

The glasshouse here (see p49) is known for cultivating various plants.

6 Ullapool
MAP C3

Delightful grid-plan village with Gaelic street names, boat trips, ferries to the Western Isles, a museum and the dream-world Assynt Mountains. Visit Corrieshalloch Gorge en route.

7 The Road to Applecross
MAP D2

To get to this small coastal village, you'll drive on pure adrenaline – the road climbs 750 m (2,000 ft) in steep zigzags to the Pass of the Sheep. Even they have to hold on tight. The scenery – with views across to Isle of Skye – is magnificent, and from here the more gradual descent into Applecross begins.

8 Timespan
MAP C5 ▪ Helmsdale ▪ (01431) 821 327 ▪ Adm ▪ www.timespan.org.uk

Well worth a visit to understand the effect of the 19th-century Clearances, which even today is visible throughout the north.

9 Dornoch Cathedral
MAP C4

Madonna chose it for her wedding and 16 earls of Sutherland requested it for their burials; Dornoch is an impressive 13th-century cathedral (now the parish church).

10 Loch Morar
MAP E3 ▪ www.lochmorar.org.uk

This enormous loch is 12 miles (18 km) long and offers great fishing, walking and wildlife watching – otters, sea eagles and golden eagles, and its own monster, Morag.

Places to Eat and Drink

1 Inverlochy Castle
MAP E3 ■ Torlundy, Fort William ■ (01397) 702 177 ■ £££

Many culinary awards have been bestowed upon the restaurant of this prestigious hotel. It boasts three dining rooms, a lavish set menu (of modern British cuisine) and a lengthy wine list.

2 Old Pines
MAP E3 ■ Spean Bridge ■ (01397) 712 324 ■ ££

Conscientiously organic, devoted to sourcing local ingredients and a member of the "slow food" movement, this little restaurant has earned a big name.

3 Airds Hotel
MAP E3 ■ Port Appin, Appin ■ (01631) 730 236 ■ £££

A country hotel restaurant with crisp, white table linen and candlelight, and a reputation for serving the best of Scottish produce.

4 The Mustard Seed
MAP D4 ■ 16 Fraser St, Inverness ■ (01463) 220 220 ■ ££

With its stylish interior and riverside location, the Mustard Seed produces some of the finest modern Scottish cuisine in the Highlands.

5 Applecross Inn
MAP D2 ■ Applecross, Wester Ross ■ (01520) 744 262 ■ £

Spectacularly located beyond Britain's highest mountain pass, this pub overlooks Isle of Skye. Local seafood is served, and there is also live music some evenings.

6 Summer Isles Hotel
MAP C3 ■ Achiltibuie, Ross-shire ■ (01854) 622 282 ■ ££

Enjoy a relaxed atmosphere while dining at the bar, which is dog-friendly. The restaurant serves more formal meals. Expect dishes such as monkfish tail with bacon, or baked halibut with parmesan crumb.

PRICE CATEGORIES

For a three-course meal for one with half a bottle of wine (or equivalent meal), taxes and extra charges.

£ under £30   ££ £30–60   £££ over £60

7 The Ceilidh Place
MAP C3 ■ 14 West Argyle St, Ullapool ■ (01854) 612 103 ■ ££

Hotel-restaurant-bar and vibrant entertainment venue. Everything from a snack to a feast, plus live music and dance aplenty.

8 Clachaig Inn
MAP E3 ■ Glencoe ■ (01855) 811 252 ■ www.clachaig.com ■ ££

A legendary haunt of walkers, this hotel offers a wide range of food but is best known for its bar – Clachaig Inn is as essential to Highland trekkers as a first Munro.

9 Plockton Shores
MAP D3 ■ 30 Harbour St, Plockton ■ (01599) 544 263 ■ ££

The fruits of the west coast are served up with love and aplomb, on the shores of beautiful Loch Carron.

10 Crannog Seafood Restaurant
MAP E3 ■ Town Pier, Fort William ■ (01397) 705 589 ■ www.crannog.net ■ ££

Fresh seafood, a panoramic loch view and generous helpings. The atmosphere is warm and welcoming, and the service efficient.

Crannog Seafood Restaurant

See map on p116

TOP 10 West Coast Islands

More than 600 islands lie scattered along Scotland's Atlantic coastline, from seabird-clustered eyots to the landmasses of Skye, Mull, Lewis and Harris. The West Coast Islands represent escapism at its best and amply repay the effort of reaching them with the distinctive lifestyles and hospitality of island folk. Regular ferries run all year, and special "island-hopping" fares are available.

Celtic cross, Islay

WEST COAST ISLANDS

0 km   40
0 miles   40

Port of Ness
North Tolsta
Isle of Lewis
Stornoway
Lochinver
Hushinish
Tarbert
Ullapool
Tigharry
Uig
Kinlochewe
Portree
Dunvegan
Stilligarry
Skye
Kyle of Lochalsh
Daliburgh
Inverie
Barra
Small Isles
Arisaig
Coll
Ardmolich
Tobermory
Iona and Staffa
Isle of Mull
Colonsay and Oronsay
Jura
Sanaigmore
Craighouse
Islay
Machrihanish
Outer Hebrides
Inner Hebrides
The Minch
The Little Minch
North Channel
A830
A83
A890

1 Top 10 Sights
see pp122–5

1 Places to Eat and Drink
see p127

1 The Best of the Rest
see p126

1 Islay
MAP F2–G2 ■ Tourist info: (01496) 305 165

A thriving island with eight distilleries *(see pp62–3)* producing peaty malts. Bowmore, the island's capital, has an unusual circular church, designed to deprive the devil of corners in which to hide. Britain's most impressive 8th-century Celtic cross can be found at Kildalton. More than 250 species of birds have been spotted on Islay's varied landscapes.

2 Jura
MAP F2 ■ Tourist info: (01496) 305 165

The wildest and least visited of all the Hebridean islands. Overrun by red deer and dominated by its central hills, the Paps, Jura has been little affected by modernity: a single road links the ferry port and the main settlement, Craighouse. If you revel in solitude and rugged scenery, the walks are tremendous.

Red deer, Jura

Colourful seafront houses of Tobermory, Mull

3 Mull
MAP E2–F2 ■ Tourist info: (01680) 812 377; www.mullwildlife.co.uk

Matching Skye for beauty if not for size, Mull is the second largest of the Inner Hebrides. Don't miss the prize gardens at Torosay Castle (accessible by miniature railway from Craignure) or the imperious Duart Castle. A tour of the island must include side trips to Iona and Staffa, and Calgary Beach will stop you in your tracks. Tobermory is the place to unwind – its colourful seafront is a classic postcard scene. The Mishish pub there often has live music.

4 Colonsay and Oronsay
MAP F2 ■ Tourist info: Bowmore, Islay; (01496) 305 165

Colonsay has provided farmland and shelter to people since at least the Bronze Age, and many of their tombs and standing stones remain. Old traditions persist here, and Colonsay is still a strong crofting (see p124) and fishing community. Wild flowers and birds thrive on this terrain, but it is the coastline, with its mix of sprawling and secretive beaches, that lures most visitors. Check the tides and walk out to the adjacent little island of Oronsay, with its ruined priory; its Christian roots go back as far as Iona's.

5 Iona and Staffa
MAP F2–E2 ■ Boats for Staffa leave from Fionnphort; www.staffatours.com ■ Tourist info: Mull (01680) 812 377

A sparkling island of white-sand beaches, Iona has an active crofting community. Visitors come in their hundreds daily in summer to visit the famous restored abbey (avoid 10am–4pm for a chance of peace). It was here that St Columba came in 563 to establish a missionary centre (see p38). Staffa contains Scotland's greatest natural wonder: Fingal's Cave, formed by thousands of basalt columns, which inspired German composer Felix Mendelssohn to pen his famous *Hebrides Overture*.

Altar inside the Iona Abbey

6 Coll
MAP E2 ■ Tourist info: Mull; (01680) 812 377

Wild flowers, migrant birds, otters, standing stones, active crofts, a castle and a surfeit of beaches contribute to making this a particularly varied and delightful island.

Breachacha Castle, Coll

7 Small Isles
MAP D2–E2 ■ Tourist info: Fort William; (01397) 701 801

While Canna and Muck are home to traditional farming communities, Rum was once the private playground of a rich industrialist; you can see his incredible fantasy home, Kinloch Castle, as well as wander the island's towering mountains. Eigg was a landmark community buyout, and the islander-owners now run a crafts shop and tours. Their ceilidhs *(see p43)* are legendary. The Sgurr of Eigg, a sugarloaf spur, yields fabulous views.

Callanish Stones, Isle of Lewis

CROFTING

Crofts are unique to the Highlands and Islands. They are small parcels of agricultural land, worked in addition to other sources of income. There are around 17,000 today, and grants now ensure their continuation. But in the mid-19th century, crofters were denied basic rights and suffered great abuse and hardship at the hands of unscrupulous landlords.

8 Isle of Lewis
MAP C2 ■ Tourist info: Stornoway; (01851) 703 088

Although geographically one island, the northern half is called Lewis and, the southern half, Harris. Together, they are world-famous for producing tweed. One thing you absolutely must see is the spectacular 4,500-year-old stone circle known as the Callanish Stones, which resonates with a deep sense of spirituality. Arnol has an engaging traditional "blackhouse" (blackened by smoke) and Carloway a fine stone fort. Harris is more mountainous. Driving the "Golden Road" reveals the best scenery; stop at the stunning Luskentyre beach, where the miles of white sands and blue-green water could almost make you believe that you are in Australia.

Plane on Cockle Beach, Barra

⑨ Barra
MAP D1 ■ **Tourist info:**
Stornoway; (01851) 703 088
This small isle encapsulates all the charm of the Hebrides: scintillating beaches, the culture of the Gaels, tranquillity and road-priority to sheep. No matter how you arrive, it will make a deep impression: planes land on the sands of Cockle Beach, while ferries sail into a delightful bay where the 11th-century Kisimul Castle poses on an island of its own. A soothing place to unwind.

⑩ Isle of Skye
Mountainous, misty and magical, Skye *(see pp26–7)* is an island of dramatic scenery, with an ancient castle, an idolized distillery and plenty more attractions.

TWO DAYS AROUND MULL

▶ MORNING

Leave **Oban** *(see p106)* on the 9:50am ferry, which arrives on **Isle of Mull** *(see p123)* at 10:40am. Book your tickets ahead *(0800 066 5000; www.calmac.co.uk)*.

You might want to spend the day on a wildlife tour, as the island is home to eagles, otters and red deer. Mull Wildlife, for instance, can meet you off the ferry. Otherwise head for Duart Castle, 13th-century home of the Macleans (a coach service connects with some mid-morning ferries, check with Calmac for the "Duart Excursion"). After exploring the castle and gardens, have lunch in their tearoom.

AFTERNOON

There are plenty of options for walks on Mull or you can drive to Calgary Bay to see the stunning white shell beach. Alternatively, make for Tobermory, the picture-postcard fishing port that is the island's main town. There are plenty of places to eat and to stay.

MORNING

Set off early to get to Fionnphort, to catch the 9:45am boat trip to **Staffa** *(see p123)*, where you can see **Fingal's Cave** *(see p70)* and the island's famous puffins. You'll be back within 3 hours, and can then pick up the quick ferry to the magical island of **Iona** *(see p123)*. Visit the **Abbey** *(see p56)*, wander its shores and enjoy its serenity. Return in time to catch the last ferry *(7pm in summer, but earlier in winter)* from Craignure back to Oban.

See map on p1

The Best of the Rest

1 Arran
MAP G3 ■ Tourist info: (01770) 303 774

Long a favourite of Glaswegians, Arran is often described as "Scotland in miniature". Goat Fell is its craggy core, while the surrounds of Brodick Castle offer more forest-path walks.

2 Tiree
MAP E1 ■ Tourist info: Mull (01680) 812 377

Well-established on the surfers' circuit, this flat island not only boasts some of the finest Atlantic rollers on its beaches, but also claims the highest number of sunshine hours in the whole of Britain.

3 The Uists and Benbecula
MAP C1–D1 ■ Tourist info: Stornoway (01851) 703 088

A string of islands connected by causeways, with huge expanses of beaches on the west and rocky mountains on the east. This is also a wonderful trout fishing area.

4 Gigha
MAP G2 ■ www.gigha.org.uk

An exceptionally fertile island ("Isle of God"), which produces gourmet cheeses and tender plants and flowers, especially in the much-acclaimed Achamore Garden.

5 Lismore
MAP E3 ■ Tourist info: Oban (01631) 563 122

Situated in splendid scenery, this once important church island is now a quiet holiday retreat. Green and fertile, its name is said to mean "great garden".

6 Easdale
MAP E3 ■ Nr Oban
■ Tourist info: (01631) 563 122

This former slate quarry has been transformed into a picturesque village. Surrounded by holes and fragmented rocks, it is bizarre and fascinating – a living museum.

7 Summer Isles
MAP C3 ■ Tourist info: Ullapool (01854) 612 486

The Summer Isles are a small cluster of islands in Loch Broom. They offer solitude and stupendous views of the magnificent arena of the Coigach mountains.

8 Kerrera
MAP E3 ■ Tourist info: Oban (01631) 563 122

A popular place for yachts to berth, this green, hilly island is ideal for walking, with clear views to Mull and the finest outlook on Oban.

9 Eriskay
MAP D1 ■ Tourist info: (01851) 703 088

The real-life scene of the *Whisky Galore* wreck in 1941, this is the dream island of the Hebrides. With beaches, crofts, hills – everything is just how the romantic would have it.

10 Luing
MAP F3 ■ Nr Isle of Seil
■ Bicycle hire: (01852) 314 274

As it is not famous for anything other than its defunct slate quarry, you should have this isle to yourself. Pretty, and easy to tour by bicycle, it makes a perfect day trip from Oban.

Lismore Lighthouse

Places to Eat and Drink

PRICE CATEGORIES

For a three-course meal for one with half a bottle of wine (or equivalent meal), taxes and extra charges.

£ under £30   ££ £30–60   £££ over £60

① Three Chimneys

MAP D2 ■ Colbost, Dunvegan, Skye ■ (01470) 511 258 ■ www.three chimneys.co.uk ■ £££

Since opening in 1985, this sublime cottage restaurant (see p65) has embraced its remote location, to create a romantic setting with an international reputation.

② Digby Chick

MAP B2–C2 ■ 5 Bank St, Stornoway, Isle of Lewis ■ (01851) 700 026 ■ www.digbychick.co.uk ■ ££

Bustling, child-friendly bistro by day; candle-lit restaurant by night. Making the most of fresh local seafood and top-quality Scottish steak, book ahead for the good-value early bird menu.

③ Langass Lodge

MAP C1 ■ Loch Eport, Isle of North Uist ■ (01876) 580 285 ■ ££

One of the finest dining experiences in the Hebrides. The magical menu takes in the freshest of local seafood, game and beef.

④ The Douglas Bistro

MAP G3 ■ Isle of Arran ■ (01770) 302 968 ■ ££

This eatery offers a modern yet classic take on bistro-style dining. It serves delicious steaks and local seafood, complemented by the superb island views.

⑤ Jura Hotel

MAP F2 ■ Craighouse, Jura ■ (01496) 820 243 ■ ££

Quaint old coastal hotel. In any one evening you are likely to meet most of Jura's inhabitants. Simple food in the scenery of the gods.

⑥ Scarista House

MAP C1 ■ Sgarasta Bheag, Isle of Harris ■ (01859) 550 238 ■ ££

This restaurant keeps things simple with a compact and bijou menu. The locally sourced food is sensational and the view is stunning.

Scarista House

⑦ Gannet Restaurant

MAP E2 ■ Coll Hotel, Ariangour, Coll ■ (01879) 230 334 ■ ££

Waterfront restaurant serving fresh seafood landed on the island. Try the local mussels in garlic and white wine or the roasted halibut.

⑧ The Mishnish

MAP E2 ■ Main St, Tobermory, Mull ■ (01688) 302 500 ■ www.mishnish.co.uk ■ ££

Celebrated pub on Tobermory's seafront. Always bustling with locals and visitors. Regular live music.

⑨ Kinloch Lodge Hotel

MAP D2–3 ■ Sleat, Skye ■ (01471) 833 333 ■ www.kinloch-lodge.co.uk ■ £££

Enjoy the food at this delightful hotel, set at tranquil spot on Skye. The five-course set dinner menu features Black Isle lamb or local sea trout. Best to book in advance.

⑩ Café Fish

MAP E2 ■ Tobermory, Mull ■ (01688) 301 253 ■ ££

Popular bistro located on the pier where much of its seafood is landed. Produce is locally sourced and the bread is homemade.

See map on p122

🔟 The Far North

Don't let the remoteness of the Far North deter you, for it is the emptiness itself that bestows upon the visitor a sense of wonder and privilege. The dazzling beaches along the northern coastline are a surprise to many, while further north still are the former Viking strongholds of Orkney and Shetland.

Orkney's land is green and fertile, and it contains one of the greatest concentrations of prehistoric remains in Europe. Shetland, on the other hand, is a much wilder frontier, festooned with millions of seabirds, and islanders who celebrate their Viking roots with a blazing fire festival, Up Helly Aa, in January.

Great skua, Handa Island

THE FAR NORTH

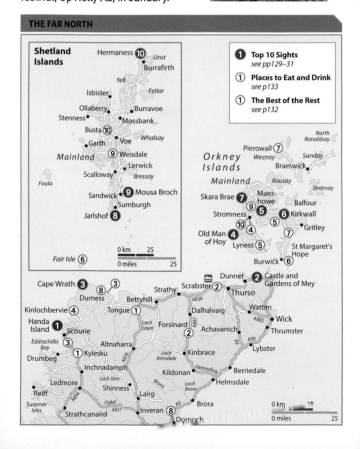

	Top 10 Sights
	see pp129–31

	Places to Eat and Drink
	see p133

	The Best of the Rest
	see p132

Shetland Islands

Hermaness ⑩ — Unst
Burrafirth
Yell — Fetlar
Isbister
Ollaberry — Burravoe
Stenness — Mossbank
Busta ⑩
Garth — Voe — Whalsay
Mainland ⑨ Weisdale
Scalloway — Lerwick
— Bressay
Sandwick ⑨ Mousa Broch
— Sumburgh
Jarlshof ⑧
Foula
Fair Isle ⑥

0 km   25
0 miles   25

Orkney Islands
Pierowall ⑦ — Westray — Sanday
North Ronaldsay
Braeswick
Mainland — Rousay — Stronsay
Skara Brae ⑦ — Maes-howe ⑨
Balfour
Stromness ⑨ ⑤ ⑥ Kirkwall
Old Man ④ ⑩ ④ ⑤ — Gritley
of Hoy — Lyness ⑤ ⑦
St Margaret's Hope
Burwick ⑥

Cape Wrath ③ — ③
Durness — Strathy — Scrabster ② — Dunnet — ② Castle and Gardens of Mey
Kinlochbervie ④ — Bettyhill — Thurso
Handa ① — Tongue ① — Dalhalvaig — Watten
Island ⑧ — Loch Loyal — Forsinard ② — A882 — Wick
Scourie ③ — Achavanich — A99 — Thrumster
Eddrachillis Bay — Altnaharra — Loch Rimsdale — Kinbrace — Lybster
Drumbeg ① Kylesku — Kildonan — Berriedale
Inchnadamph — Helmsdale — Helmsdale
Ledmore — Loch Shin — Loch Brora
Reiff — Shinness — Lairg
Summer Isles — Oykel — Inveran ⑧ — Brora
Strathcanaird — A837 — Dornoch

0 km   25
0 miles   25

1 Handa Island
MAP B3 ■ Ferry: (07780) 967 800 ■ Scottish Wildlife Trust: www.scottishwildlifetrust.org.uk

Once populated by a hardy people who elected a queen and ran their own parliament, Handa was evacuated when the potato crop failed in 1847. Now it is a fantastic colony of seabirds that live here. Of particular note are the belligerent arctic and great skuas, kittiwakes, razorbills and the largest assembly of guillemots – numbering 66,000 – in Britain. A ferry from Tarbet will take you to this island.

2 Castle and Gardens of Mey
MAP B5 ■ A836 Thurso–John O'Groats ■ (01847) 851 473 ■ Adm ■ www.castleofmey.org.uk

On the windswept Caithness coast is the UK's most northerly mainland castle, the Castle of Mey. Since 1952, the late Queen Elizabeth, the Queen Mother, lovingly restored the castle and gardens – her own personal taste is very apparent. The castle and grounds are now in trust for the benefit of the people of Caithness.

3 Cape Wrath
MAP B3 ■ Ferry: (01971) 511 246; open May–Sep

This is the most northwesterly point on the British mainland. Perched high on a clifftop stands a Stevenson lighthouse (1827); below, the ocean pounds

Cape Wrath Lighthouse

the rocks in a mesmerizing display of the Atlantic's strength. At Clo Mor, 8 km (5 miles) eastwards, are the highest cliffs on mainland Britain at 281 m (900 ft). The cape is reached by ferry from Keoldale Pier on the Kyle of Durness, and a minibus runs to the lighthouse in summer.

4 Old Man of Hoy, Orkney
MAP A5 ■ Bike hire: www.orkneycyclehire.co.uk

This sandstone pinnacle rising 137 m (449 ft) from the sea is the most famous stack in Britain. It seems to change colour constantly as the light varies, and never fails to mesmerize. Climbers have scaled its precipitous face. The Scrabster–Stromness ferry deviates to give passengers a view, but its best angle is from land. Hire bikes at Stromness and cycle to Rackwick Bay (on the way visit the Dwarfie Stane, a hollow rock), then it's a 2-hour round trip on foot.

Old Man of Hoy, seen from the westernmost point of Hoy, Orkney

The Neolithic cairn of Maeshowe on Orkney

5 Maeshowe, Orkney

MAP A5 ■ (01856) 851 266
■ Open Apr–Sep: 10am–5pm daily
(Oct–Mar: to 4pm) ■ Adm (free for
HES members)

This magnificent stone burial chamber, built around 2700 BC, is a World Heritage Site. Stoop low and walk through the entrance tunnel, carefully aligned with the solstice sun, and enter the greatest concentration of Viking graffiti ever discovered. Norsemen plundered the treasure but left the walls with a wealth of runes describing the kind of boasts and grumbles that people still make today. Opt for the torchlit tour.

6 Kirkwall, Orkney

MAP A5 ■ Tourist info: (01856)
872 856 ■ Palaces: (01856) 871 918;
open Apr–Sep; adm ■ Museum:
(01856) 873 535

The capital of Orkney is a town of twisted streets, ancient buildings and the constant comings and goings of ferries. Most striking is the enormous red and yellow St Magnus's Cathedral, built in the 12th century and still going strong. Nearby are the ruins of the bishop's and earl's palaces. The town museum is excellent, and many shops in the city sell an extensive range of Orcadian jewellery.

7 Skara Brae, Orkney

MAP A5 ■ (01856) 841 815
■ Open Apr–Sep: 9:30am–5:30pm
daily; Oct–Mar: 10am–4pm daily
■ Adm (free for HES members)

Another World Heritage Site, and one that predates the Egyptian pyramids. In 1850, a storm revealed some ruins in the sands. Archaeologists excavated and were astonished to find a 5,000-year-old Stone Age village, which had been abandoned so suddenly that most of the rooms and furnishings were left intact. Today, you can see the stone beds and sideboards of these Neolithic people, and discover how and what they cooked. A visitor centre explains.

8 Jarlshof, Shetland

MAP B1 ■ (01950) 460 112
■ Open Apr–Sep: 9:30am–5:30pm
daily (Oct–Mar: call for open times)
■ Adm (free for HES members)

This warren of underground (but roofless) chambers represents not one but at least five periods of settlement. The oval-shaped houses are Bronze Age; the Iron Age added the broch and wheelhouses; the Picts established their own dwellings; the Vikings erected long houses, and a farm was created in medieval times. This archaeological site, close to the soaring bird-cliffs of Sumburgh Head, is exceptional.

Jarlshof, Shetland

⑨ Mousa Broch, Shetland

MAP B2 ▪ Boat trips: (07901) 872 339; open Apr–mid-Sep daily (weather permitting); www.mousa.co.uk

Around 500 BC the Iron Age people began building defensive forts called brochs. Masterfully designed, these double-skinned walls of dry stones were raised into circular towers, with an elegant taper at their waists. Remains of brochs are scattered across northern Scotland but Mousa is the best preserved. You can only reach it by boat, and then must climb 13 m (43 ft) to the open parapet.

Mousa Broch, Shetland

⑩ Hermaness National Nature Reserve, Shetland

MAP A2 ▪ Unst ▪ (01595) 693 345 ▪ Best visiting times: mid-May–late Jul

When you look from here to Muckle Flugga lighthouse, you're gazing at the northernmost tip of Britain. Aside from the view, the cliff-edged reserve is a favourite breeding ground for bonxies (great skuas). Alongside these pirates (they steal food from other seabirds), there are gannets, razorbills, red-throated divers and a large gathering of tammy nories (puffins).

A DAY ON ORKNEY

▶ MORNING

Start the morning from the flagstoned village of **Stromness** *(see p132)* and head out on the road to **Skara Brae**. The roads turn and undulate on rolling pasture but the way is well signposted, which is a pity as Orkney is a delightful place to get lost in.

You'll need 2 hours to do the Neolithic remains justice, as well as fitting in a visit to Skaill House and stocking up on sweet treats such as fudge and ice cream in the shop.

Drive on to the great ancient stone circle known as the **Ring of Brodgar** *(see p132)*, and also visit the roadside standing stones of Stenness.

So far you've only covered 20 km (12 miles). Time for lunch as you make your way to the Maeshowe Visitor Centre.

AFTERNOON

After lunch, take a tour inside Neolithic **Maeshowe**. It's dark inside, and a guide lights up the runes with a torch. Drive on to **Kirkwall**. Visit the cathedral and the museum, and walk the town's charming streets, or stop for a coffee.

In the evening, dine at **The Commodore Restaurant & Bar** *(Map A5; Main Street, Holm, Orkney; 01856 781 788; closed L, Sun–Thu)*.

Orkney is also a delightful place to cycle and it's easy to hire bicycles. The car route described above makes a lovely day's cycle ride if you return to Stromness after Maeshowe.

See map on p128 ←

The Best of the Rest

1 Eas A'Chual Aluinn Fall, nr Kylesku

MAP B3 ▪ Take a boat from Kylesku; (01971) 502 231; open Mar–Oct

Eas A'Chual Aluinn is Britain's highest waterfall. It drops 200 m (658 ft) at the end of Loch Glencoul.

2 Forsinard Flows

MAP B4 ▪ (01641) 571 225
▪ Visitor centre: open Apr–Oct
▪ www.rspb.org.uk

The great peatland, known as the Flow Country, offers walks among rare plants, insects and birds.

3 Smoo Cave, Durness

MAP B4 ▪ www.smoocavetours.weebly.com

Remarkable natural cavern beside the sea. You can walk in a little way, but a floodlit boat tour is best.

4 Pier Arts Centre, Stromness

MAP A5 ▪ www.pierartscentre.com

There is a collection of British fine art here. Most works were created in the 1930s and 1940s by avant-garde artists.

5 Scapa Flow Visitor Centre, Hoy, Orkney

MAP A5 ▪ (01856) 791 300 ▪ Closed for restoration ▪ www.scapaflow.co.uk

An exploration of the bay of Scapa Flow, where, in 1917, the captive German Navy scuttled 74 ships.

6 Fair Isle, Shetland

MAP B1
▪ www.fairisle.org.uk

Famous for knitted patterns and as a haven of traditional crafts, this remote island has awesome cliff scenery and birdlife (from May to mid-August, puffins are the big draw). The ferry is weather-dependent, so be prepared for a wait.

Façade of the Italian Chapel, Orkney

7 Churchill Barriers and Italian Chapel, Orkney

MAP A5 ▪ Lamb Holm, nr Kirkwall ▪ Chapel: open Nov–Mar: 10am–1pm daily (Apr & Oct: to 4pm); May & Sep 9am–5pm daily (Jun–Aug: to 6:30pm) ▪ Adm

These causeways were built in World War II by Italian prisoners of war, who were also for the exquisite chapel.

8 Dornoch

MAP C4

This attractive market town features a 13th-century cathedral, a museum of local history, plenty of shops and cafés as well as a long sandy beach.

9 Ring of Brodgar, Orkney

MAP A5 ▪ Nr Stromness
▪ www.stromnessorkney.com

An atmospheric prehistoric site of 36 slabs raised to form a circle. There are taller (but fewer) standing stones nearby at Stenness.

A puffin catches dinner, Fair Isle

10 Stromness, Orkney

MAP A5 ▪ Tourist info: www.stromnessorkney.com

Stromness is a quaint town of flagstoned streets with a museum that draws on the Orcadian connection with the Hudson Bay Shipping Company.

Places to Eat and Drink

PRICE CATEGORIES

For a three-course meal for one with half a bottle of wine (or equivalent meal), taxes and extra charges.

£ under £30 ££ £30–60 £££ over £60

---

1 Tongue Hotel
MAP B4 ▪ Tongue ▪ (01847) 611 206 ▪ ££

A characterful old hotel, the low prices of which belie the quality of exotic Highland fare served. The best of local produce is used with imagination and flair.

2 The Captain's Galley
MAP B5 ▪ The Harbour, Scrabster ▪ (01847) 894 999 ▪ Closed Sun & Mon ▪ £££

Stylish restaurant in an exposed-brick former ice house. Serves all different kinds of fish, fresh from the morning's catch. Book in advance.

3 Eddrachilles Hotel, Scourie
MAP B3 ▪ Badcall Bay, Scourie ▪ (01971) 502 080 ▪ ££

Among trees on a ragged coastline, this fine old hotel has a stone-walled dining room where local sourced food is served. A long conservatory, too, for catching the sun.

4 Kinlochbervie Hotel
MAP B3 ▪ Kinlochbervie ▪ (01971) 521 275 ▪ £

Somewhat stark, but it more than makes up for it with its good views and simple value-for-money food. Hill lamb, venison, salmon and local seafood are favourites. Good wines.

5 The Foveran
MAP B5 ▪ St Ola, Kirkwall ▪ (01856) 872 389 ▪ Oct–Apr: call to check D times; book ahead ▪ ££

Renowned restaurant serving dishes such as fillet of Orkney steak and North Ronaldsay mutton. It offers great views over Scapa Flow.

6 The Skerries Bistro
MAP B5 ▪ Nr Burwick ▪ (01856) 831 605 ▪ Closed Mon & Wed L, Sat & Sun D ▪ ££

Set in a glass building with superb views of the Pentland Firth, this lovely restaurant serves local produce such as hand-dived scallops.

7 Pierowall Hotel, Orkney
MAP A5 ▪ Pierowall, Westray ▪ (01857) 677 472 ▪ £

Come here for the best fish and chips in the isles – probably in Scotland. Nothing fancy, but simple home cooking and plenty of choice.

8 Cocoa Mountain
MAP B3 ▪ 8 Balnakeil, Durness ▪ (01971) 511 233 ▪ £

An unlikely location for a world-class chocolatier, but one not to miss. On offer are delicious artisan truffles and hot chocolate, as well as a selection of coffees and teas. A bonus is the beautiful views of Loch Criospol

Chocolate truffles, Cocoa Mountain

9 Mill Café, Shetland
MAP B1 ▪ Weisdale ▪ (01595) 743 843 ▪ Closed Mon ▪ £

In this renovated old mill, combine the visual delights of the Bonhoga Gallery with delectable snacks: marinated herring, smoked salmon, organic quiches.

10 Busta House, Shetland
MAP A1 ▪ Busta, Brae ▪ (01806) 522 506 ▪ ££

This historic Shetland hotel (see p151) also boasts a revered and reasonably priced restaurant. The tastiest lamb on the island is found here, along with seafood dishes, including particularly good scallops and halibut.

See map on p128

Streetsmart

Jeffrey Street and the roofs
of Old Town, Edinburgh

Getting To and Around Scotland

Arriving by Air

Scotland has four international airports: **Edinburgh**, **Glasgow**, **Prestwick** and **Aberdeen**. There are also regional airports in Dundee, Orkney, Shetland, Inverness and the Outer Hebrides. Edinburgh Airport is 11 km (7 miles) from the city centre. There are buses to the city centre, every 10 to 15 minutes, that take around 30 minutes, as well as trams that take 35 minutes. Taxis are available too. There are direct flights from the USA, China and Europe, as well as good domestic links to London. Connecting flights go to Orkney, Wick, the Isle of Lewis and Shetland.

Glasgow Airport is 13 km (8 miles) from the city centre. The best way to get to the city is by shuttle bus (every 10 minutes, journey 25 minutes). Taxis are also available. You can get a bus to Skye via Loch Lomond and Fort William. There are direct flights from Canada and the USA, as well as good domestic links to London. Connecting flights go to Barra, Benbecula, Campbeltown, Orkney, Shetland, Islay, the Isle of Lewis and Tiree.

Prestwick is 48 km (30 miles) from Glasgow city centre. The airport has its own railway station and trains run four times an hour to Glasgow Central station (twice an hour on Sunday). Buses run approximately every 30 minutes to the city centre. The airport has links to some European destinations such as Pisa, Rome and Malaga.

Aberdeen Airport is 11 km (7 miles) from the city centre. The Jet Connect bus runs to the city (31 minutes). Buses also run to Montrose and Stonehaven. Taxis are also available. The nearest railway station to the airport is Dyce and taxis and buses connect with trains. The airport has direct links to European destinations such as Amsterdam, Paris and Gdansk. There are connecting routes to Orkney, Shetland, the Isle of Lewis and Wick.

Arriving by Train

St Pancras International is the London terminus for **Eurostar**, linking the UK with the continent. From here there are quick links to Kings Cross and Euston, where there are trains to Edinburgh and Glasgow.

Arriving by Coach

Day and night **National Express** services operate out of many major cities. Reliable and cheaper than trains, journeys by coach are longer. The main station in Edinburgh is just off St Andrew's Square in the New Town; Glasgow's is opposite the Royal Concert Hall at the east end of Sauchiehall Street. The Megabus M20, that can be booked through **Megabus**, runs between Edinburgh and London Victoria. There are two services a day (8 hours 30 minutes).

Arriving by Road

The M6, A68 and partially coastal A1 are the main road routes into Scotland, with the former for Glasgow, and the latter two for Edinburgh. There are no border controls.

Arriving by Sea

There is no ferry service between Scotland and continental Europe, but **P&O** sails between Hull and Rotterdam and Zeebrugge, and DFDS sails between Newcastle and Amsterdam. Ferry services by **Stena Line** and P&O operate between the Irish ports of Belfast and Larne to Scotland's southwest coast.

Travelling by Train and Tram

Scotland boasts one of the most scenic railway routes in the world. The West Highland Line *(see p52)*, runs between Glasgow and Oban or Glasgow and Fort William and Mallaig. Book tickets with **ScotRail** or **West Coast Railways**. The Borders Railway runs between Tweedbank and Edinburgh. A Spirit of Scotland Pass is available on **Britrail**. There is also a **ScotRail** Central Scotland Rover ticket and a Highland Rover. All offer unlimited train travel for a certain number of days. Other train tickets are available through **Trainline** and **National Rail Enquiries**.

Edinburgh's tram links the city centre with the airport. It runs along Princes Street with stops at Waverley and Haymarket stations. The Glasgow Subway system comprises a single loop.

Travelling by Bus

The largest bus provider is **Scottish Citylink**. City buses don't give change. **Rabbie's Trail Burners** and **MacBackpackers** are two renowned minibus-and-hostel tour companies.

Travelling by Car

Driving is a convenient way to tour Scotland; but parking charges mean that city centres are best explored on foot or by public transport. Roads are good and there are no tolls. Single-track roads have "passing places", and when two cars meet, the car nearest to one should reverse and pull into it, or stop opposite. The Highway Code, available in bookshops, details all road regulations. While driving it is compulsory to wear seatbelts, illegal to use mobile phones and drink driving limits are strict: no more than 50 mg of alcohol per 100 ml of blood. Car hire firms such as **Avis**, **Europcar** and **Hertz**, are at major airports.

Travelling by Taxi

Taxis are regulated and legally obliged to display a licence number. City taxis (**City Cabs**, in Edinburgh, and **Glasgow Taxis**) should be metered but unmetered cars operate in remote areas – ask for the fare before you get in.

Travelling by Ferry

Caledonian MacBrayne works the majority of west coast routes. Smaller companies, such as **Ferry Savers**, also run ferries to and around Scotland's 99 inhabited islands.

Travelling by Bicycle

Long-distance cycle routes and mountain bike trails are available on **Forestry Commission** land, plus a number of city cycle networks. Bike transport is possible on most trains. Faster, long-distance services require pre-booking.

Travelling on Foot

With a network of marked footpaths, Scotland is great for walking. There are walking festivals too. Check **Visit Scotland**, **Scotways**, **Ramblers** and the **Scottish Mountaineering Club** for information.

DIRECTORY

ARRIVING BY AIR
Aberdeen
w aberdeenairport.com
Edinburgh
w edinburghairport.com
Glasgow
w glasgowairport.com
Prestwick
w glasgowprestwick.com

ARRIVING BY TRAIN
Eurostar
w eurostar.com

ARRIVING BY COACH
Megabus
w uk.megabus.com
National Express
w nationalexpress.com

ARRIVING BY SEA
P&O
w poferries.com
Stena Line
w stenaline.co.uk

TRAVELLING BY TRAIN AND TRAM
Britrail
w britrail.net

National Rail Enquires
c (08457) 484 950
w nationalrail.co.uk
Scotrail
w scotrail.co.uk
Trainline
w trainline.com
West Coast Railways
w westcoastrailways.co.uk

TRAVELLING BY BUS
MacBackpackers
w macbackpackers.com
Rabbies Trail Burners
w rabbies.com
Scottish Citylink
w citylink.co.uk

TRAVELLING BY CAR
Avis
w avis.co.uk
Europcar
w europcar.co.uk
Hertz
w hertz.co.uk

TRAVELLING BY TAXI
City Cabs (Edinburgh)
c (0131) 228 1211
w citycabs.co.uk

Glasgow Taxis
c (0141) 429 7070
w glasgowtaxis.co.uk

TRAVELLING BY FERRY
Caledonian MacBrayne
w calmac.co.uk
Ferry Savers
w ferrysavers.co.uk

TRAVELLING BY BICYCLE
Forestry Commission
w scotland.forestry.gov.uk

TRAVELLING ON FOOT
Ramblers
w ramblers.org.uk/scotland
Scottish Mountaineering Club
w smc.org.uk
Scotways
w scotways.com
Visit Scotland
w visitscotland.com

Practical Information

Passports and Visas

Visitors from outside the European Economic Area (EEA) and Switzerland need a valid passport to enter the UK; EEA and Swiss nationals can use identity cards. Those from the European Union (EU), the USA, Canada, Israel, Australia and New Zealand don't need a visa.

Visitors from other countries should check whether a visa is required at the **UK Visas and Immigration** website or with the British Embassy in their country of origin.

A number of countries including **New Zealand**, **USA** and **Canada** have embassies in Edinburgh and can be approached if you lose your passport, need a visa or wish to extend your stay.

Customs and Immigration

Visitors from EU states can bring unlimited quantities of most goods into the UK for personal use without paying duty. Exceptions include illegal drugs, offensive weapons, endangered species and some types of food and plants. For information about allowances from within and outside the EU, visit the UK government's website. If you need regular medicine, bring adequate supplies or a prescription with you.

Travel Safety Advice

Visitors can get up-to-date travel safety information from the **UK Foreign and Commonwealth Office**, the **US Department of State** and the **Australian Department of Foreign Affairs and Trade**.

Travel Insurance

Use an insurance policy that covers cancellation or curtailment of your trip, healthcare and theft or loss of money and baggage. Emergency treatment is usually free from the **National Health Service**, and there are reciprocal arrangements with other EEA countries, Australia, New Zealand and some others (or check www.gov.scot/Topics/Health/Services/Overseas-visitors). A specialist car, medicines and repatriation are costly. Residents of EEA countries must carry an up-to-date European Health Insurance Card (EHIC), which allows treatment in Britain for free or at reduced cost.

Health

Vaccinations are not required before visiting. Hospitals with 24-hour emergency services in Scotland include **University Hospital Ayr**, **Borders General Hospital** in Melrose, **Dumfries and Galloway Royal Infirmary**, **Victoria Hospital** in Fife, **Aberdeen Royal Infirmary**, **Glasgow Royal Infirmary**, **Royal Infirmary of Edinburgh** and **Belford Hospital** in Fort William.

Pharmacies are open in business hours, some until late, and can give advice on minor ailments. Boots is a large chain with branches all over Scotland, including one on Princes Street in Edinburgh, open until 7pm during the week (8pm Thursday) and until 6pm Sunday. Hotels are usually able to suggest local dentists and doctors.

Personal Security

Scotland is quite safe, but assaults and muggings can take place. Take sensible precautions: avoid dark, deserted places; use your intuition about entering less salubrious areas; and don't flaunt money or valuables. Unattended items may cause a security alert, especially at airports or railway/bus stations. Women travelling solo should stick to busy areas at night and use only licensed taxis displaying an identification disc. Insure possessions and leave passports and tickets in the hotel safe. Report thefts to the police.

Mountain Safety

If you plan to walk or climb in the mountains, be sure you are well prepared for sudden changes in weather; a blizzard can rage on the summit even if the lower slopes are sunny. Check the **Mountain Weather Information Service** before you go.

Use good walking boots, waterproof jacket and trousers, hat, gloves, fleece, map and compass. Take a simple first-aid kit, whistle, mobile phone as well as a GPS. Tell someone where you intend to walk and the time you expect to return. In an emergency, contact **Mountain Rescue**.

Emergency Services

For emergency **police**, **fire**, **ambulance** services, or emergency **mountain rescue**, dial 999 (or 112). For medical help or non-emergency situations, dial 111. These numbers are free on any public phone.

Travellers with Specific Needs

Visit Scotland's *(see p141)* website has information for those with specific needs.

Modern sights tend to be accessible, but historic buildings may not be. Phone ahead to check.

Capability Scotland is Scotland's largest organization and **Tourism for All** is the UK's central source of travel information.

Disability Rights UK lists accommodation. **Seagull Trust Cruises** runs canal boats that are specifically designed for the disabled on the Forth (Edinburgh) and Caledonian (Inverness)

canals. Hertz supplies hand-controlled vehicles, suitable for drivers with full upper-body mobility. Disabled parking bays are widespread but you must display an official sign. The AA produce a *Disabled Travellers' Guide* and have a **Disability Helpline** for members.

Other sources that offer useful advice are **Can Be Done**, **Action on Hearing Loss** and the **Royal National Institute for the Blind**.

DIRECTORY

PASSPORTS AND VISAS

Canadian
MAP F5 ■ 5 St Margarets Rd, Edinburgh
🆆 canadainternational. gc.ca

New Zealand
MAP K4 ■ 5 Rutland Sq, Edinburgh
🆆 mfat.govt.nz

UK Visas and Immigration
🆆 gov.uk/browse/visas-immigration

US
MAP Q2 ■ 3 Regent Terrace, Edinburgh
🅲 (0131) 556 8315
🆆 uk.embassy.gov

TRAVEL SAFETY ADVICE

Australian Department of Foreign Affairs and Trade
🆆 dfat.gov.au/ smartraveller.gov.au

UK Foreign and Commonwealth Office
🆆 gov.uk/foreign-travel-advice

US Department of State
🆆 travel.state.gov

TRAVEL INSURANCE

National Health Service
🆆 nhs.uk

HEALTH

Aberdeen Royal Infirmary
Foresterhill, Aberdeen
🅲 (0345) 456 6000

Belford Hospital
Belford Rd, Fort William
🅲 (01397) 702481

Borders General Hospital
Huntlyburn, Melrose
🅲 (01896) 826000

Dumfries and Galloway Royal Infirmary
Cargenbridge, Dumfries
🅲 (01387) 246246

Galloway Community Hospital
Dalrymple St, Stranraer
🅲 (01776) 707707

Glasgow Royal Infirmary
MAP V2 ■ 84 Castle St
🅲 (0141) 211 4000

Royal Infirmary of Edinburgh
51 Little France Crescent, Old Dalkeith Rd, Edinburgh
🅲 (0131) 536 1000

Victoria Hospital
Hayfield Rd, Kirkcaldy
🅲 (01592) 643355

MOUNTAIN SAFETY

Mountain Rescue
🆆 mountainrescue scotland.org

Mountain Weather Information Service
🆆 mwis.org.uk

EMERGENCY SERVICES

Ambulance, fire, police, mountain rescue
🅲 999 (or 112)
🅲 111 (non emergency)

TRAVELLERS WITH SPECIFIC NEEDS

The AA Helpline
🅲 (0800) 262050
🆆 theaa.com

Action on Hearing Loss
🅲 (0808) 808 0123
🆆 actiononhearingloss. org.uk

Can Be Done
🅲 (020) 8907 2400
🆆 canbedone.co.uk

Capability Scotland
🅲 (0131) 337 9876
🆆 capability-scotland. org.uk

Disability Rights UK
🆆 disabilityrightsuk.org

Royal National Institute for the Blind
🅲 (0303) 123 9999
🆆 rnib.org.uk

Seagull Trust Cruises
🆆 seagulltrust.org.uk

Tourism for All
🅲 (0845) 124 9971
🆆 tourismforall.org.uk

Currency and Banking

Britain's currency is the pound sterling (£), divided into 100 pence (p). Scotland has three banks: Royal Bank of Scotland (RBS), Bank of Scotland and the Clydesdale Banks. Each produces different notes which can be met with confusion or suspicion if you try to use them south of the border, though they are usually accepted. Scottish notes come in £5, £10, £20, £50 and £100 denominations. Coins come as 1p, 2p, 5p, 10p, 20p, 50p, £1 and £2.

There's no limit on the amount of cash you can bring into the UK. Banks tend to offer the best exchange rates and are generally open 9am–5pm Monday to Friday. Some open on Saturday. In remote areas you may find a mobile bank parked and open for business. Bureaux de change work longer hours in the main cities and at airports. They are regulated and their rates are displayed along with commission charges. Cash machines (ATMs) can be found throughout the country. Always shield your pin from view.

Credit cards are widely accepted across Scotland but many small shops, cafés and most B&Bs deal only in cash. Visa and MasterCard are the most commonly accepted cards.

Telephone and Internet

Wi-Fi hot spots and internet cafés are common in the cities.

Most towns have cafés with Wi-Fi. The majority of libraries and hotels provide internet access.

Public phones are found throughout Scotland. Some accept credit cards, but most require a phonecard, which can be purchased at many shops. To call an operator, dial 100 or the International Operator (155). For free directory enquiries, call (0800) 118 3733.

When calling a UK number from abroad, dial the access code (0044), then omit the first zero from any standard number. To call abroad from the UK, dial 00 followed by the country code (1 for the USA and Canada, 61 for Australia).

Check before leaving home whether your mobile phone will work in the UK. Consider buying a UK SIM card, or use a VoIP service, such as Skype (skype.com). There are still pockets in the Highlands and Islands without mobile coverage.

Postal Services

Standard post is handled by the **Royal Mail**. There are post offices throughout Scotland, some in supermarkets or other stores. Larger post offices will open from 9am to 5:30pm on weekdays and until 12:30pm on Saturdays. You can also buy stamps in shops.

TV, Radio and Newspapers

Television channels have proliferated in recent years: BBC1, BBC2, BBC3 and BBC4 remain in public ownership, with

distinctive broadcasting output in Scotland. Radio stations such as BBC Radio Scotland carry news and travel updates. BBC nan Gaidheal broadcasts in Gaelic.

For current events and news, the free newspaper *Metro* is available at main railway stations. *The Scotsman* and *Scotland on Sunday* are Edinburgh-based broadsheets, while *The Herald* and *Sunday Herald* are Glasgow-based broadsheets. The *Evening News* (Edinburgh) and the *Evening Times* (Glasgow) are main evening papers. *The Press and Journal* covers the north-east. The main tabloid is *The Daily Record* while *The Sunday Post* has an extremely loyal readership. *The List* magazine is the listings publication covering theatre, cinema, events, bars and restaurants. A collection of Scottish books is available at the Waterstones branch which is located at 128 Princes St, Edinburgh. It organizes various events such as book clubs as well as author readings.

Opening Hours

Most shops are open 9am–5:30pm Monday to Saturday. City shops usually open until 8pm Thursday and many now open Sunday, too. Museum and gallery times vary widely, so check before starting out. Last admission to many attractions is 30 minutes before closing. There are three key holiday periods: Hogmanay (New Year), Easter and July–August. The main holidays in

Scotland are 1–2 January, Good Friday (March/April), the first and last Monday in May, first Monday in August and 25–26 December. Local holidays include the "Trades" in early July in Edinburgh, and the "Glasgow Fair", later in July.

Time Difference

Scotland operates on Greenwich Mean Time (GMT) which is 1 hour behind Continental Europe Time and 5 hours ahead of US Eastern Seaboard Time. The clock advances 1 hour during "British Summer Time", spanning the last Sunday in March until the last Sunday in October. In summer, Scotland enjoys longer days than the rest of the UK, while the days are shorter in winter.

Electrical Appliances

The electricity supply is 240 volts AC. Plugs are of a three-square-pin type. Buy an adaptor at your departure airport. Most hotels have shaver sockets in the bathroom.

Driving

EEA citizens can drive in the UK, so long as they carry their full and valid licence, registration and insurance documents. Other foreign nationals can drive a car or motorcycle for 12 months, on the same terms. Be sure to get insurance.

Weather

Scotland has a highly variable weather pattern. The east is drier than the west, but rain can occur throughout the year, and heavy snowfalls are possible in winter – seldom longer than a few days, except in the hills. Summer temperatures average 15–22° C (59–72° F); winter temperatures 1–7° C (34–45° F).

The **Met Office** website carries up-to-date, detailed forecasts.

Visitor Information

Visit Scotland provides good general information and has a website – an excellent place to start planning your trip. Visit Britain operates information offices in many cities around the world. Scotland's major visitor information centres are in Edinburgh and Glasgow, and there are regional tourist offices, some open year-round, others open during the summer months only.

Tickets for the **Edinburgh International Festival**, **Edinburgh Fringe** and the **Edinburgh Military Tattoo** can be booked from their respective ticket offices. Many of Scotland's oldest buildings are under the custodianship of **Historic Environment Scotland** or the **National Trust for Scotland**.

DIRECTORY

POSTAL SERVICES

Edinburgh Post Office
MAP N3 ▪ 5/6 Princes Mall, Waverley Bridge

Glasgow Post Office
MAP T3 ▪ 136 West Nile St

Royal Mail
w royalmail.com

NEWSPAPERS

The Herald
w heraldscotland.com

The Scotsman
w scotsman.com

WEATHER

Met Office
w metoffice.gov.uk

VISITOR INFORMATION

Edinburgh Festival Fringe Box Office
MAP N3 ▪ 180 High St
c (0131) 226 0026
w tickets.edfringe.com

Edinburgh Information Centre
MAP N3 ▪ 3 Princes St
c (0131) 473 3868

Edinburgh International Festival
w eif.co.uk

Edinburgh Tattoo
MAP N3 ▪ 33-34 Market St
w edintattoo.co.uk

Glasgow Information Centre
MAP F4 ▪ 156a/158 Buchanan St, Glasgow
c (0141) 556 4083

Historic Environment Scotland
w historicenvironment. scot

Hub Ticket Office
MAP M4 ▪ Castlehill, Edinburgh
c (0131) 473 2000
w thehub-edinburgh.com

National Trust for Scotland
w nts.org.uk

Visit Scotland
w visitscotland.com

Trips and Tours

An open-top sightseeing bus is a great way to get to know Glasgow and Edinburgh. Some allow you to hop on and hop off at leisure. The main operators are **City Sightseeing** and **Edinburgh Bus Tours**. It is also well worth taking a boat trip on one of the many crafts operating in Scotland. There are a range of trips from Anstruther in Fife to the **Isle of May** (a National Nature Reserve famed for its birdlife), to a gentle cruise on the Caledonian Canal.

Shopping

Scotland offers a wide range of souvenirs, from local crafts, jewellery and clothing to food and drink. Prices can vary, so it pays to shop around. VAT (Value Added Tax) is charged at 20 per cent. End-of-season sales and outdoor markets offer the best bargains, but beware of inferior products. Edinburgh's popular department store is **Jenners** on Princes Street but there is also a branch of **Harvey Nichols** on St Andrew Square. The main fashion stores are on George Street, while **The Italian Centre** in Glasgow's Merchant City, and **Princes Square** off Buchanan Street, have many high-end stores.

For individual arts, crafts, books and food, make for Stockbridge or Bruntsfield, just outside Edinburgh city centre, or the area around the Byers Road in Glasgow.

Scotland's tartans come in hundreds of patterns and dozens of forms, notably the kilt. These are complex garments to make and require several weeks' work. Tweed for suits, jackets and skirts also comes in a wide variety of designs. Shetland and the Borders are well-known sources of woollens, but there is no need to restrict your search here, as design has excelled in the last two decades. Visit mills all over Scotland. The **Textile Trail** has details of everything from weavers to kiltmakers.

Packaged food make excellent presents to take home. Smoked salmon, kippers (smoked herring), haggis, Tablet (a delicious Scottish fudge), Dundee cake and shortbread are popular souvenirs. When it comes to alcoholic drinks, take home Moniack country wines, Drambuie liqueur or Edinburgh gin. By far the most popular drink is whisky, which is available in standard bottles, miniatures or special presentation cases. Unfortunately, it is highly taxed and often cheaper outside the UK. You can purchase it at distilleries, at the Scotch Whisky Heritage Centre, in supermarkets and off-licences across the country.

Look out for jewellery in Scotland, a flourishing area of innovative design. Orkney produces an astonishing array of quality jewellery. Popular traditional designs feature Celtic-knot work and other interwoven patterns, and make use of the Cairngorm, an orange semiprecious stone.

Among companies that produce luxury handmade toiletries in Scotland, **Arran Aromatics** stands out. Their high-quality soaps and creams all use local, natural and eco-friendly ingredients.

Galleries selling art are found all over Scotland. Edinburgh Printmakers deals in contemporary fine art printmaking. Stills (also in Edinburgh) is a long-established gallery, and Street Level (in Glasgow) is a dynamic photography gallery.

Dining

Scotland offers cuisines from across the globe. Italian, Indian and Chinese are perennial favourites with Scots and generally offer good value: Glasgow is famed as one of the great "curry capitals" of Britain. Vegetarians will usually find at least one option on any Indian, Chinese or Italian menu. Glasgow and Edinburgh have the best choice of international cuisine, plenty of fine-dining and Michelin-starred restaurants, as well as pubs serving bar meals and snacks. Set lunches and pre-theatre deals often represent good value.

For seafood lovers, there are numerous options. Argyll and the islands are noted for their excellent seafood. Make sure to try fresh fish and chips. The Arbroath Smokie – fresh haddock smoked over hardwood chips – is a delicacy from the coastal town of Arbroath. The Arbroath Smokie Trail lists places where you can try this tasty traditional dish.

In the major cities, Scots generally have dinner between 7pm and 9pm and lunch between 12:30pm and 2pm, when pubs, cafés and fast-food restaurants fill up. Outside the cities, dinner is generally eaten earlier and last orders for food are taken by 8pm in pubs, hotels and restaurants – check beforehand. It is customary to tip at 10 per cent of the bill, but service is usually included in the price.

Restaurant reviews can be found in *The List* and **OpenTable**, the latter offering online reservations and some special deals. **Taste of Scotland** samples all kinds of places and lists those of a good or high standard. It also features food festivals, events and farmers' markets.

Accommodation

Hotels vary from luxurious country houses to budget chains. Guesthouses and B&Bs offer rooms in private homes with breakfast included. They offer opportunities for meeting locals. Self-catering flats, cottages, eco-lodges and caravans are cost-effective for families and groups. Organizations such as **The Landmark Trust** and the **National Trust for Scotland** offer self-catering accommodation in historic properties such as lighthouses and castles. The **Scottish Youth Hostels Association** (SYHA) operates many hostels. Take your membership card and travel with a sheet (some require a sleeping bag). There are numerous independent hostels with their own websites, that do not require membership. There's no shortage of camping and caravan sites which are usually of a high standard and set in beautiful locations. Lesser facilities may be offered in remoter areas but the prices will be lower and the views even better. **The Mountain Bothies Association** is a charity that looks after over 100 unlocked "bothies" (simple wooden, iron or stone huts). Set in remote areas, they usually have a sleeping platform, table, seats and a fireplace. They are free, but donations are accepted.

Whether you're staying in a modest B&B or a luxurious country house hotel, make sure to have a full Scottish breakfast. Hotels usually offer tea between 3pm and 5pm in the afternoon. If you wish to make the most of Scotland's fresh air and have a picnic, many hotels and B&Bs will happily prepare you one. Head for a loch side, a deserted beach or a country park.

If you plan to stay for longer than two nights in any one place, many hotels, guesthouses and B&Bs give discounts, as well as offerspecial weekly rates. You can tour Scotland without reservations but it is generally best to book, especially in high season. The best deals at budget hotel chains are found online well in advance. Book accommodation at Visit Scotland information centres

---

DIRECTORY

TRIPS AND TOURS

City Sightseeing
- city-sightseeing.com
- citysightseeing glasgow.co.uk

Edinburgh Bus Tours
- edinburghtour.com

Isle of May Ferry
- isleofmayferry.com

SHOPPING

Arran Aromatics
- arran.com

Harvey Nichols
MAP N2 ■ 30–34 St Andrew Sq, Edinburgh
- harveynichols.com

The Italian Centre
MAP U3 ■ 7 John St, Glasgow

Jenners
MAP N3 ■ 47 Princes St, Edinburgh
- houseoffraser.co.uk

Princes Square
MAP T3 ■ 48 Buchanan St, Glasgow
- princessquare.co.uk

Textile Trail
- ourscottishborders.com

DINING

The List
- food.list.co.uk

OpenTable
- opentable.co.uk

Taste of Scotland
- taste-of-scotland.com

ACCOMMODATION

The Landmark Trust
- landmarktrust.org.uk

Late Rooms
- laterooms.com

Mountain Bothies Association
- mountainbothies. org.uk

National Trust for Scotland Holidays
- nts.org.uk/holidays

Scottish Youth Hostels Association
- hostellingscotland. org.uk

Places to Stay

PRICE CATEGORIES

For a standard, double room per night (with breakfast if included), taxes and extra charges.

£ under £100   ££ £100–200   £££ over £200

Edinburgh's Luxury Hotels

Waldorf Astoria Edinburgh

MAP L3 ■ Princes St & Lothian Rd ■ (0131) 222 8888 ■ www.waldorf astoria3.hilton.com ■ ££

With its very formal Pompadour restaurant and the relaxed dining area, the Waldorf (formerly the Caledonian) is something of an institution. Opulence, indulgence and a superb Guerlain spa, with a pool and steam room.

Balmoral

MAP N2–3 ■ 1 Princes St ■ (0131) 556 2414 ■ www. roccofortehotels.com ■ £££

The most prestigious of Edinburgh's old-school hotels, right on Princes Street, sports two great restaurants – Michelin-starred Number One and Brasserie Prince by Alain Roux. The hotel also boasts a spa with a Finnish sauna.

The Chester Residence

MAP J3–4 ■ 9 Rothesay Pl ■ (0131) 226 2075 ■ www.chester-residence. com ■ £££

These gorgeous serviced apartments, featuring luxurious furnishings, are spread across a number of townhouses. Breakfast can be delivered to your room. For an experience like a film-star, opt for the Owners Residence that has a private cinema.

The Glasshouse

MAP P2 ■ 2 Greenside Pl, Leith Walk ■ (0131) 525 8200 ■ www.theglass househotel.co.uk ■ £££

A private rooftop garden crowns this crystal palace of contemporary design tucked beneath the classical monuments of Calton Hill. Impeccable service, good food and suites with walls of glass, allowing views across the Edinburgh rooftops to the Firth of Forth.

Kimpton Charlotte Square Hotel

MAP L3 ■ 38 Charlotte Square ■ (0131) 240 5500 ■ www.ihg.com ■ £££

Seven elegant Georgian townhouses have been transformed into a sleek and stylish hotel, decorated with dark wood and leather furnishings. The rooms and suites feature carefully chosen artworks, yoga mats and Nespresso machines. The restaurant here serves Middle Eastern cuisine.

Radisson Collection, Royal Mile

MAP N4 ■ 1 George IV Bridge ■ (0131) 220 6666 ■ www.radisson collection.com ■ £££

This eye-catching building is located on the corner of the Royal Mile and is a haven of designer chic, with rooms and suites that are individually curated – featuring fine textiles, rain showers and offering compelling city views. The roof of this hotel features bee hives, and the restaurant uses fresh local produce.

The Scotsman

MAP P3 ■ 20 North Bridge ■ (0131) 556 5565 ■ www.thescots manhotel.co.uk ■ £££

Formerly home of *The Scotsman* newspaper, this solid building has been transformed into a stylish hotel, that has, bright rooms. Superbly situated, it looks north over the New Town. The Grand Café, offers an all-day menu as well as afternoon tea.

The Witchery

MAP M4 ■ Castlehill ■ (0131) 225 5613 ■ www. thewitchery.com ■ £££

Champagne and cookies await each guest in this cocoon of romance. Bose sound systems and cable TV are the modern touches in the nine antique-filled, indulgent suites. It has an excellent restaurant, Witchery by the Castle (see p81).

Edinburgh's Boutique and Mid-Range Hotels

Apex City Hotel

MAP M4 ■ 61 Grassmarket ■ (0131) 243 3456 ■ www. apexhotels.co.uk ■ ££

This has joined its sister hotel up the road at

No. 31, with modern, simple and functional rooms, and a mix of business and family facilities (photocopying and secretarial services in the former case, cots and highchairs in the latter).

The Bonham

MAP K3 ▪ 35 Drumsheugh Gardens ▪ (0131) 226 6050 ▪ www.bespoke hotels.com ▪ ££
Created from three Victorian townhouses, The Bonham makes a chic and comfortable base. It has bold styling, with modern furnishings and a range of communication and entertainment devices (including fast Internet and DVDs). The restaurant cuisine tilts towards modern European.

DoubleTree by Hilton

MAP L5 ▪ 34 Bread St ▪ (0131) 221 5555 ▪ www. doubletree3.hilton.com ▪ ££
The most style-conscious hotel in Edinburgh. Broad sweeps of intense colour add vitality to the sharp minimalism throughout, and bedrooms and bathrooms are very well appointed and relaxing. The hotel also has a good restaurant and one of the best bars in town.

Fraoch House

MAP F5 ▪ 66 Pilrig St ▪ (0131) 554 1353 ▪ www. fraoch house.com ▪ ££
A lovely Victorian building whose period features have been fused with contemporary design to produce a clean and vibrant modern look. Delicious Scottish cooked breakfasts will set you up for a day of sightseeing.

Inverleith Hotel

MAP K5 ▪ 5 Inverleith Terrace ▪ (0131) 556 2745 ▪ www.inverleith hotel.com ▪ ££
Victorian town house hotel, close to the Royal Botanic Garden *(see p48)*. Try for the four-poster room, or the Georgian self-catering apartment in the New Town.

Malmaison

MAP K5 ▪ 1 Tower Pl, Leith ▪ (0131) 285 1487 ▪ www.malmaison.com ▪ ££
As its name suggests, Malmaison looks to France for inspiration, and provides a winning mix of good brasserie food and contemporary styling in its rooms – and wonderful bathrooms. Nicely set on the quay with all its restaurants.

Rabble

MAP M2 ▪ 55a Frederick St ▪ (0131) 622 7800 ▪ www.rabbleedinburgh. co.uk ▪ ££
You'll find very stylish rooms at Rabble, each kitted out with GHD hair straighteners and a fully-stocked Smeg fridge. Cooked breakfasts are served until noon, with takeaway bags available for those making an early start.

Edinburgh's B&Bs, Budget and Self-Catering

Castle Rock Hostel

MAP M4 ▪ 15 Johnston Terrace ▪ (0131) 225 9666 ▪ www.castlerock edinburgh.com ▪ £
Castle Rock is a lively, cheerful and well-run hostel in an excellent central location just off the Royal Mile and below Edinburgh Castle. The large common rooms have a piano and coal fire as well as free Wi-Fi. There is a sun deck that provides breathtaking city views. Amenities include a guest kitchen for self-caterers. They also feature dorms, double as well as triple rooms.

Brooks Hotel

MAP K5 ▪ 70 Grove St ▪ (0131) 228 2323 ▪ www.brooks edinburgh.com ▪ ££
Brooks is a reasonably priced, modern, bright and comfortable hotel, in a rustic stone building. In such a compact capital, none of the main sights are very far away, and either the Old Town or Princes Street can be reached within a 15-minute walk. All the rooms are fully equipped with TVs, decent beds, uncluttered decor and en-suite showers.

Georgian Apartments

MAP M2 ▪ 26 Abercromby Place ▪ (0131) 624 0084 ▪ www.georgian apartmentsedinburgh. co.uk ▪ ££
For self-catering in style, head to these two properties in leafy Abercromby Place both have a double bedroom, plus two beds in a screened-off section of the living room, a fully equipped kitchen, free Wi-Fi and free parking. There is a two-to-three-night booking policy.

Gerald's Place

MAP M1–2 ▪ **21B Abercromby Place** ▪ (0131) 558 7017 ▪ www. geraldsplace.com ▪ ££
This B&B is situated in the elegant Georgian New Town. There are just two bedrooms, each with private bathrooms and power showers.

Haymarket Hub Hotel

MAP J4 ▪ **7 Clifton Terrace** ▪ (0131) 347 9700 ▪ www. haymarkethubhotel.com ▪ ££
This smart budget chain in the West End is located along the tram route. The chain has conveniently located hotels with 24-hour security, power showers and free Wi-Fi.

Ibis Hotel

MAP P3 ▪ **6 Hunter Square** ▪ (0131) 619 2800 ▪ www. accorhotels.com ▪ ££
Smart, neat, clean and functional hotel that makes up for in prime location (just off the Royal Mile) what it lacks in terms of space in the bedrooms and bathrooms.

Southside Guest House

MAP K5 ▪ **8 Newington Rd** ▪ (0131) 668 4422 ▪ www.southsideguest house.co.uk ▪ ££
This elegant 19th-century town house with a secluded garden and a library on each landing sports eight beautifully designed bedrooms that would not look out of place in a boutique hotel. Charming hosts provide faultless hospitality that includes locally sourced food and a complimentary Buck's Fizz cocktail with breakfast.

Glasgow's Luxury Hotels

Sherbrooke Castle

MAP Y3 ▪ **11 Sherbrooke Ave** ▪ (0141) 427 4227 ▪ www.sherbrookecastle-hotel.com ▪ ££
A baronial building in a quiet residential corner of Glasgow close to the Burrell Collection, and an easy 10-minute train ride from the city centre. The decor alternates between an upbeat, boutique look and a more traditional, somewhat stately feel.

ABode Glasgow

MAP X3 ▪ **129 Bath St** ▪ (0141) 221 6789 ▪ www.abodeglasgow. co.uk ▪ £££
A Neo-Classical 19th-century townhouse has been given a designer makeover, artfully blending Edwardian wood panelling and ironwork with a modern aesthetic look. The rooms are spacious, with big beds and pillows you could easily nest in.

Blythswood Square

MAP X3 ▪ **11 Blythswood Square** ▪ (0141) 248 8888 ▪ www.phcompany.com ▪ £££
This elegant boutique hotel on a quiet central Glasgow square boasts marble interiors and tweed furnishings. It has a bustling restaurant, a popular bar and a spa.

Hotel Du Vin

MAP Y2 ▪ **1 Devonshire Gardens, off Great Western Rd** ▪ (0141) 378 0385 ▪ www.hotel duvin.com ▪ £££
This stretch of Victorian terrace in the West End is the epitome of timeless, sophisticated luxury. The individually styled rooms are awash with deluxe fabrics and carefully selected antique furniture. With opulent bathrooms and high-tech gadgetry in the bedrooms, why venture outside the front door?

Malmaison

MAP W3 ▪ **278 West George St** ▪ (0141) 378 0384 ▪ www.malmaison glasgow.com ▪ £££
Malmaison exercises its mantra of getting the details right: large, comfortable beds, mood lighting and self-indulgent bathrooms, with power showers and baths suitable for hour-long soaks. There's a French-style brasserie in the crypt (the building is a converted church) and a gym to counterbalance all the lazing about.

Glasgow's Mid-Range and Boutique Hotels

Alexander Thomson Hotel

MAP X4 ▪ **320 Argyle St** ▪ (0141) 221 1152 ▪ www.alexander thomsonhotel.co.uk ▪ £
This modern hotel has spotless contemporary standard rooms. It is in a convenient city centre location close to Glasgow Central railway station.

Alison Guesthouse

MAP Z3 ▪ **26 Circus Drive** ▪ (0141) 556 1431 ▪ www. thealison.co.uk ▪ £
This elegant Victorian villa, owned and maintained by a family living on the grounds, retains many of its original features. It has

comfortable rooms, an off street parking, and a large garden. Its location is conveniently close to several popular destinations in Glasgow.

The Brunswick
MAP Y4 ■ 106–108 Brunswick St ■ (0141) 552 0001 ■ www.brunswick hotel.co.uk ■ £

Housed in a smart, copper-topped building in the buzzing Merchant City area, this hotel has a modern-chic interior that is not too formal and a friendly café-bar. The rooms are well-lit with modern amenities such as flat-screen TVs and free Wi-Fi.

Apex City of Glasgow Hotel
MAP X3 ■ 110 Bath St ■ (0141) 319 4570 ■ www. apexhotels.co.uk ■ ££

Behind its curiously angular (and somewhat ugly) glass façade, the Apex offers superb value for money in a very central location. The spacious rooms have pristine facilities and boutique styling. All have Sky TV and free Wi-Fi.

Ibis Hotel
MAP W3 ■ West Regent St ■ (0141) 619 9000 ■ www. accorhotels.com ■ ££

Like its neighbour, Novotel, the Ibis isn't a prospect that gets the heart racing, but it does provide very good value, achieved through an even tighter economy of scale in the bedrooms and, particularly, in the bathrooms. The location is central, and as a place to take a shower and curl up for the night, drifting off to late-night TV, it's hard to beat for price.

Novotel
MAP W3 ■ 181 Pitt St ■ (0141) 619 9001 ■ www. accorhotels.com ■ £££

While the Novotel is unlikely to feed the mind with recollections of a truly memorable stay, it does provide simple, comfortable accommodation with inoffensive decor. Food and drink are readily at hand in the pleasant bar and restaurant.

Glasgow's B&Bs, Budget and Self-Catering

Dreamhouse Apartments
(0045) 226 0232 ■ www. dreamhouseapartments. com ■ £

In various West End locations close to Kelvingrove Park, these luxurious one- and two-bed apartments have elegant modern styling and full maid service. An excellent choice if you're staying for more than a few nights.

Glasgow Youth Hostel
MAP Z2 ■ 8 Park Terrace ■ (0141) 332 3004 ■ www. hostellingscotland.org ■ £

Although it's half an hour's walk from the city centre, Glasgow's SYHA hostel enjoys a lovely setting in an elegant and spacious Victorian mansion overlooking Kelvingrove Park, convenient for Kelvingrove Art Gallery & Museum. Some of the rooms have glorious views.

SACO
MAP Y4 ■ 53 Cochrane St ■ (0330) 202 0505 ■ www.sacoapartments. co.uk ■ £

These twelve luxury-on-a-budget one-bedroom apartments in the heart of town offer a minimum three-night stay. They are fully serviced with simple, modern furnishings.

The Alamo Guest House
MAP Z2 ■ 46 Gray St ■ (0141) 339 2395 ■ www. alamoguesthouse.com ■ ££

Art, antiques and ornate original plasterwork lend a gorgeous period atmosphere to this 19th-century townhouse in a prime West End location, just a few minutes' walk from some of Glasgow's top restaurants. Perks include posh toiletries, bathrobes and a movie library, while the more expensive rooms have garden views; the best room boasts a luxurious freestanding bathtub.

Mainland: Luxury Hotels

Knockinaam Lodge, Portpatrick
MAP H3 ■ Portpatrick ■ (01776) 810 471 ■ www. knockinaamlodge.com ■ ££

Knockinaam nestles in a romantic setting by the sea. Room rates include top-quality dinner and breakfast (see p89).

Boath House, Moray
MAP D4 ■ Auldearn, Nairn ■ (01667) 454896 ■ www. boath-house.com ■ £££

A Georgian mansion set amid gardens and woodland, this is not just a hotel but also a luxury retreat with a sauna, spa, gym, and a full range of beauty treatments, including Ayurvedic remedies. Good healthy food completes the package.

Cameron House, Loch Lomond

MAP F4 ▪ Nr Luss ▪ (01389) 310 777 ▪ www. cameronhouse.co.uk ▪ £££

An enduring favourite to which many stars hop by helicopter from Glasgow. Right on Loch Lomond, this turreted mansion has extensive leisure facilities, including a large pool, tennis courts and a marina. At mealtimes, choose between the Michelin starred dining room and the all-day Cameron Grill restaurant.

Culloden House, Inverness

MAP D4 ▪ Culloden Rd, Balloch ▪ (01463) 790 461 ▪ www.cullodenhouse. co.uk ▪ £££

Bonnie Prince Charlie stayed here (he commandeered the place in 1746) and the hosts have dined out on the story ever since. Glistening chandeliers and Adams plasterwork enhance a building of exceptional architecture. Every room at Culloden House is uniquely decorated, and there's superb dining, too.

Glencoe House, Glencoe

MAP E3 ▪ Glencoe ▪ (01855) 811 179 ▪ www.glencoe-house. com ▪ £££

This lovely 19th-century mansion, built by the governor of Canada's Hudson Bay Company, still sports much finery from the time, including marble fireplaces, parquet floors and ornate ceilings. Service is attentive but not intrusive: breakfast is served whenever you want.

Gleneagles, Auchterarder

MAP F4 ▪ Perthshire ▪ (01764) 662 231 ▪ www. gleneagles.com ▪ £££

A superb country-house resort, arguably Scotland's finest, with warm personal service and old-fashioned style. Leisure activities available at Gleneagles include cycling, riding, archery and a fantastic spa, not to mention a world-class golf course (see p57). The resort is also home to one of Scotland's best and most famous restaurants, the French-influenced Andrew Fairlie (see p95).

Inverlochy Castle, Fort William

MAP E3 ▪ Torlundy ▪ (01397) 702 177 ▪ www.inverlochy castlehotel.com ▪ £££

This has been among Scotland's elite for so long, it has become the benchmark for excellence. The hotel is set against a stunning landscape of surrounding mountains and has sumptuous decor. The King of Norway presented the dining-room furniture as a gift, and he wouldn't be disappointed with what's served upon it.

Isle of Eriska Hotel, Ledaig

MAP E3 ▪ Benderloch, nr Oban ▪ (01631) 720 371 ▪ www.eriska-hotel.co.uk ▪ £££

Isle of Eriska Hotel sees extravagant luxury on an island sanctuary near the mouth of Loch Linnhe. The hotel defines good living (see p71).

Kinloch House, Blairgowrie

MAP E5 ▪ Blairgowrie ▪ (01250) 884 237 ▪ www. kinlochhouse.com ▪ £££

With all the key features of a 19th-century Scottish country house, Kinloch House is the perfect place to experience the country's history. There are individually decorated rooms. Wander in the beautiful walled garden containing hundreds of roses, and explore the dignified public rooms including a venerable portrait gallery.

Mainland: Mid-Range and Boutique Hotels

Ednam House Hotel, Kelso

MAP G6 ▪ Bridge St ▪ (01573) 224 168 ▪ www. ednamhouse.com ▪ ££

Overlooking the River Tweed, this classic Georgian mansion is a major draw for its rooms as well as the restaurant. The building itself retains period features and makes a comfortable base to explore the glorious and scenic countryside of the Borders.

Fauhope, Melrose

MAP G5 ▪ Gattonside, Melrose ▪ (01896) 823 184 ▪ www.fauhope house.com ▪ ££

Built in 1897, this secluded house has enchanting views to the River Tweed and Eildon Hills. It is tastefully decorated and staff display impeccable hospitality. You will find rich colours, antiques and a bottle of sherry in the rooms. For comfort and price, this ranks among the best in the Borders.

Glen Clova Hotel, Glen Clova

MAP E5 ■ Nr Kirriemuir ■ (01575) 550 350 ■ www. clova.com ■ ££
This excellent old hotel offers fine food, character and relaxation in spades, in the best of central Scotland's scenery. Ideally located for keen walkers, this establishment offers offers a wide range of options to suit everyone.

Glenfinnan House Hotel, Glenfinnan

MAP E3 ■ Bridge St ■ (01397) 722 235 ■ www.glenfinnan house.com ■ ££
An imposing 18th-century pine-panelled stately home which overlooks Loch Shiel. Excellent value, the rooms vary in price according to the views. Glenfinnan House has good home cooking and a bar where folk musicians often gather.

Kinkell House, Cromarty Firth

MAP C4–D4 ■ Conon Bridge, nr Dingwall ■ (01349) 864 641 ■ www.kinkellhouse hotel.com ■ ££
In a delightful country house, which catches the sunrise over the Cromarty Firth and the sunset over Ben Wyvis, this hospitable hotel is beautifully furnished and decorated. It offers great value, and makes a comfortable base for exploring the Black Isle.

Macdonald Aviemore Resort

MAP D4 ■ Aviemore, Inverness ■ (0344) 879 9152 ■ www.macdonald hotels.co.uk ■ ££
This resort, located in the highlands, has three hotels and 18 luxurious self-catering woodland lodges – so offering something for all budgets.

Old Pines Hotel, Spean Bridge

MAP E3 ■ (01397) 712 324 ■ www.oldpines. co.uk ■ ££
This Scandinavian-style hotel in a single-storey house, with easy wheel chair access, has a play area for children and views to Ben Nevis. Dinner at the restaurant *(see p121)* can be included with accommodation rates.

Riverwood Strathtay, Pitlochry

MAP E4 ■ Nr Pitlochry ■ (01887) 840 751 ■ www.riverwood strathtay.com ■ ££
A stylish retreat with four acres of lawns and woods beside the River Tay with its good trout fishing. Each room is decorated in a chic and neutral Arts and Crafts style. A minimum two-night stay is required to book.

Cringletie House, Peebles

MAP G5 ■ Edinburgh Rd ■ (01721) 725 750 ■ www.cringletie.com ■ £££
Built in the mid-19th century on the site of a much older property, this charming house is set in its own grounds. Rooms are individually

designed and there's also a converted cottage with a hot tub.

Mainland: Guesthouses and B&Bs

Dalshian Guest House, Pitlochry

MAP E5 ■ Old Perth Rd ■ (01796) 472 173 ■ www. dalshian.co.uk ■ £
A wonderful 18th-century guesthouse set within an acre of secluded woodland and gardens that offer a quiet retreat beyond the fringes of Pitlochry. Rooms are attractive and modern and there is a comfortable guest lounge replete with a wood burning stove.

Fiorlin, Melrose

MAP G5 ■ Abbey St ■ (01896) 822 984 ■ www. melroseaccommodation. co.uk ■ £
Close to the abbey and set inside its own walls in a quiet cul-de-sac, this B&B offers very comfortable self-contained accomodation, with shops and a number of restaurants nearby. The owners are especially attentive to the needs of their guests.

Glencoe Youth Hostel, Ballaculish

MAP E3 ■ (01855) 811 219 ■ www.syha.org.uk ■ £
This quiet hostel is situated in one of the most spectacular glens in Scotland, on the doorstep of some of the best year-round walking and climbing. Compare notes with other ramblers at the famous nearby Clachaig Inn, where the day's mountaineering tales are swapped every night.

Glenfinnan Sleeping Car, Glenfinnan
MAP E3 ▪ Glenfinnan Station Museum ▪ (01397) 722 295 ▪ www.glenfinnan stationmuseum.co.uk ▪ £

The most unusual beds in Scotland are to be found in a disused railway sleeping coach, which now stands at Glenfinnan Station Museum. It sleeps 10, and you can pay by the night or hire the whole wagon by the week. All-day light meals are served in an adjacent coach. All aboard!

Globe Inn, Aberdeen
MAP D6 ▪ 13 North Silver St ▪ (01224) 641 171 ▪ www.the-globe-inn.com ▪ £

The bedrooms a the Globe Inn are located above one of Aberdeen's best pubs, so this is not a place for early-to-bed guests, but the value and location – bang in the city centre – can't be beaten. Hearty breakfast will set you up for the day. Parking on the street needs to be paid for.

Rowardennan Youth Hostel, nr Drymen
MAP F4 ▪ Rowardennan ▪ (01360) 870 259 ▪ £

This is one of the busiest youth hostels in Scotland owing to its superb location, which is on the banks of Loch Lomond and also on the West Highland Way walking path *(see p52)*. Ben Lomond sweeps up at the back and at the front is a private beach. Rowardennan is very popular with families. Definitely book ahead.

Rua Reidh Lighthouse, Gairloch
MAP C3 ▪ Melvaig, Gairloch ▪ (01445) 771 263 ▪ www.stayatalight house.co.uk ▪ £

Built in 1912 by a cousin of Robert Louis Stevenson, this idyllic lighthouse offers some magnificent views over the Minch to Skye and the Western Isles. There are basic private rooms and hostel beds available.

Beach Cottage B&B, Inverness
MAP D4 ▪ 3 Alturlie Point ▪ (01463) 231 676 ▪ www.beachcottage inverness.co.uk ▪ ££

It's not unusual to see dolphins swimming in the Moray Firth from this renovated 18th-century fisherman's cottage, and rooms have been designed to make the most of the stunning views.

Five Pilmour Place, St Andrews
MAP F5 ▪ St Andrews, nr Old Course ▪ (01334) 478 665 ▪ www.5pilmour place.com ▪ ££

The best of a string of pleasant guesthouses by St Andrews' Old Course, the rooms here have a modern boutique feel, thanks to high-quality furnishings and various comforts. Guests can enjoy the walled garden. An excellent breakfast is included in the room rate.

Mackay's, Durness
MAP B4 ▪ Sutherland ▪ (01971) 511 202 ▪ www. visitdurness.com ▪ ££

This long-standing family-run hotel has smart wood-and-slate decor in its log-fired lounge, and stylishly decorated rooms. It's welcoming as well as immaculate, and enjoys wonderful views of the surrounding countryside.

Easter Dunfallandy Country House, Pitlochry
MAP E4–5 ▪ Perthshire ▪ (01796) 474 031 ▪ www. dunfallandy.co.uk ▪ £££

In an idyllic location overlooking the Tummel Valley, this small self-catering property has five bedrooms and can accommodate up to 12 people. Enjoy inexpensive rural living, where the day begins with a hearty Highland breakfast. A maximum of two dogs are allowed by prior arrangement.

Island Accommodation

Berneray Youth Hostel, Berneray
MAP C1 ▪ North Uist ▪ (0845) 293 7373 ▪ www.gatliff.org.uk ▪ £

A charming thatched cottage, Berneray Youth Hostel provides somewhat primitive accommodation in the most stunning location. Plus it's just four hops to the beach.

Lochranza Youth Hostel, Arran
MAP G3 ▪ Lochranza ▪ (01770) 830 631 ▪ Closed 3 Mar–28 Oct ▪ £

In a beautiful location below Arran's mountains, and close to the sea and an ancient castle, rests Lochranza Hostel. Secluded in a woodland garden, this old country house makes a great base for exploring the island. It is close to a bus route and has its own small shop.

Salen Hotel, Mull

MAP E2 ■ Salen, Aros
■ (01680) 300 324 ■ www.
salenhotelmull.co.uk ■ £
Centrally located and close
to Ben More, this informal
hotel offers comfortable
rooms and superb views.
The dining room boasts
panoramic vistas, and
there are hearty dishes on
the menu. Pets welcome.

Ardhasaig House, Isle of Harris

MAP C2 ■ Ardhasaig
■ (01859) 502 500 ■ www.
ardhasaig.co.uk ■ ££
Set by one of the most
picturesque roads in the
isles, this 1904 house has
been completely refur-
bished, while retaining
certain period features.
With light decor, simple
furnishings and captivat-
ing views, this B&B is of
the highest calibre. There
is the option of a four-
course set menu for
dinner. A self-catering
cottage is also available.

Broad Bay House, Lewis

MAP B2 ■ Isle of Lewis
■ (01851) 820 990 ■ Closed
Mar–Oct ■ www.broad
bayhouse.co.uk ■ ££
Beautifully located beside
a sweeping sandy beach,
this guesthouse is only
a short drive north of
Stornoway. The contem-
porary rooms are styled in
natural wood, with a glut of
hi-tech facilities, including
iPod docking stations.

Busta House Hotel, Shetland

MAP A1 ■ Brae ■ (01806)
522 506 ■ www.busta
house.com ■ ££
A remote and peaceful
country house hotel, this
is one of the great get-
away-from-it-all retreats

in Scotland. Busta House
delivers first-class quality
in every respect and detail.

The Colonsay Hotel, Colonsay

MAP F2 ■ Isle of Colonsay
■ (01951) 200 316 ■ www.
colonsayholidays.co.uk
■ ££
This traditional inn, built
in 1750, has always been
an island social centre
and often hosts live
music. Rooms are bright
and simple, and guests
can enjoy a garden, ter-
race and library. Curl
up with a good book
and enjoy some fine sea
views over the neighbour-
ing island of Jura.

Glenegedale, Islay

MAP F2 ■ Isle of Islay,
Argyll ■ (01496) 300 400
■ www.glenegedalehouse.
co.uk ■ ££
Glenegedale is a classic
whitewashed Hebridean
house in a glorious setting
overlooking Laggan Bay
and the Irish coast. Every
room here has been indi-
vidually decorated and
there is a full range of
modern facilities and
quaint touches, such as
chocolates left on the
pillow, bowls of fresh fruit
and roaring peat fires in
the colder months. An
Cuan, run by the same
owners, is a self catering
property located nearby,
with spectacular Laggan
Bay views from its ele-
vated position.

Pennygate Lodge

MAP E2–3 ■ Craignure,
Mull ■ 01680 812 333
■ www.pennygatelodge.
scot ■ ££
A Georgian manse, set in
its own grounds, overlooking Craignure Bay. The
rooms are decorated with

antiques, fresh flowers
and artworks. Some also
offer a view of the sea.

Viewfield House, Skye

MAP D2 ■ Portree
■ (01478) 612 217 ■ Closed
Apr–Oct ■ www.viewfield
house.com ■ ££
A rambling building set
in 81,000 sq m (97,000 sq
yards) of woodland garden,
Viewfield House has been
a family house since the
early 19th century. Guests
are made very welcome
and, if they so wish, can
choose to dine together in
the Victorian dining room.

Calgary Farmhouse

MAP E2 ■ Calgary, Mull
■ (01688) 400 256 ■ www.
calgary.co.uk ■ £££
Close to Calgary Bay, one
of Mull's most beautiful
white-sand beaches, this
converted farm complex
offers a range of self-
catering accommodation,
from a cosy studio flat for
two to the magnificent
oak-beamed Hayloft,
which sleeps up to eight
people comfortably. A
minimum of three-days'
booking is essential.

Flodigarry Country House, Skye

MAP C2 ■ Staffin, Isle of
Skye ■ (01470) 552 203
■ www.hotelintheskye.
co.uk ■ £££
Situated close to the sea
and below the Trotternish
Ridge stands this 19th-
century mansion, which
retains many period fea-
tures and a fireplace that
is lit in winter. The views
from the sunny conser-
vatory are marvellous.
Flodigarry Country House
is an affordable retreat
with a growing, glowing
reputation for good food.

For a key to hotel price categories see p144

General Index

Acknowledgments

Author
Alastair Scott is a freelance travel writer and photographer based in Edinburgh and on the Isle of Skye.

Additional contributors
Rebecca Ford, Neil Wilson

Publishing Director Georgina Dee

Publisher Vivien Antwi

Design Director Phil Ormerod

Editorial Michelle Crane, Rachel Fox, Freddie Marriage, Fíodhna Ní Ghríofa, Scarlett O'Hara, Erin Richards, Sally Schafer

Cover Design Maxine Pedliham, Vinita Venugopal

Picture Research Susie Peachey, Ellen Root, Lucy Sienkowska, Oran Tarjan

Cartography Reetu Pandey, Suresh Kumar, James Macdonald

DTP Jason Little, George Nimmo

Production Linda Dare

Factchecker Christian Williams

Proofreader Nikky Twyman

Indexer Helen Peters

First edition created by Blue Island Publishing, London

Revisions Hansa Babra, Stuti Tiwari Bhatia, Neha Chander, Rebecca Flynn, Sumita Khatwani, Shikha Kulkarni, Rahul Kumar, Rada Radojicic, Anuroop Sanwalia, Anupama Shukla, Priyanka Thakur, Rachel Thompson, Vaishali Vashisht, Tanveer Zaidi

Commissioned Photography Joe Cornish, Andy Crawfor, Alex Havret, Ian O'Leary, Rough Guides/Helena Smith, Clive Streeter, Linda Whitwam

Picture Credits
The publisher would like to thank the following for their kind permission to reproduce their photographs:

Key: a-above; b-below/bottom; c-centre; f-far; l-left; r-right; t-top

4Corners: SIME/Olimpio Fantuz 4b.

Alamy Images: age fotostock/Gonzalo Azumendi 63tl; The Archives 10cl; blickwinkel 7tr, 129tr; Blue Gum Pictures 129b; Mark Boulton 30bl; Douglas Carr 32cla, 56b, 107clb; David Chapman 130br; Derek Croucher 26cl; Ian G Dagnall 10bl, 116tl; Karen Debler 35cra; Dave Donaldson 49tr; eye35 67tr; D. G. Farquhar 119clb; Keith Fergus 28bl; FLPA 11br; Philip Game 98cla; Jeff Gilbert 19tr; Ross Gilmore 74tl; Dennis Hardley 30-1, 47t, 49bl, 110t, 124cla; Cath Harries 62b, Hemis fr / Rieger Bertrand 11cb, Hemis.fr / Gregory Gerault 118ca; Jan Holm 11tr; Holmes Garden Photos/Neil Holmes 92cb; imageBROKER/Jose Antonio Moreno Castellano 102tr; Imagestate Media Partners Limited - Impact Photos/Peter Thompson 27crb; Brian Jannsen 14t; John Peter Photography 35bl, 84tl, 86tl, 98b, 104-5; Kayroxby Image Scotland 15br; Geraint Lewis 39tr; Look Die Bildagentur der Fotografen GmbH/Andreas Strauss 12br; Loop Images Ltd/Cath Evans 125tl; Vincent Lowe 131cl; Matthew Clarke 54t; Niall McDiarmid 67clb; John McKenna 54cb; Paintin /Scottish National Gallery *An Old Woman Cooking Eggs* (1618) by Diego Rodriguez de Silva y Velazquez, 16bl; Photoshot 128cra; Prisma Bildagentur AG 23crb; M Ramírez 20cr; Realimage 43tr; Rolf Richardson 29bl; David Robertson 4clb; Seymour Rogansky 47br; Iain Sarjeant 109br; Scottish Mainland 59clb; Duncan Shaw 46bl; Steve Allen Travel Photography 43bl; StockImages 103ca; Ivan Vdovin 66cb; Scottish Viewpoint 31tr; David Wall 70b; Paul White - North West Highland Scotland 117br; Allan Wright 109t.

Angus Council: 94c.

Atholl Estates: Stephen Farthing 41br; Paul Booth 91tr.

At the Sign of the Black Faced Sheep: 113tl.

AWL Images (Jon Arnold & John Warburton-Lee Photography): Hemis 50-1; Tom Mackie1.

BrewDog Edinburgh: 80tr.

Bridgeman Images: Art Gallery and Museum, Kelvingrove, Glasgow/*Old Willie - The Village Worthy* (1886) Sir James Guthrie 20bl, /*The Annunciation*, (c.1490) Sandro Botticelli 21bl; © Culture and Sport Glasgow (Museums) 10crb (d); Private Collection /© Look and Learn 38cb.

Cairngorms National Park: 34bl.

City Merchant: Danielle McQuade 101cra.

City of Edinburgh Council: Alan Laughlin 78cla.

Cocoa Mountain: 133cr.

Corbis: Nathan Benn 32cb; Hemis/Christophe Boisvieux 45tl, 75br; Guido Cozzi 2tl, 8-9; JAI/Fortunato Gatto 119tl, /Mark Sykes 97tr; Loop Images/Sebastien Wasek 46cla; Hans-Peter Merten 110-1; Andy Trowbridge 132cb; VIEW Pictures Ltd /Hufton + Crow 23bl.

Crannog Cruises and Restaurant: 121br.

Crown Copyright Reproduced Courtesy of Historic Scotland: Santiago Arribas Pena 10ca, 70tl, 88tl, 106tl, 130t.

Dreamstime.com: App555 11tl, 58br; Jennifer Barrow 11cra, 28-9, 75tl, 76b; Serge Bertasius 35tr; Lukas Blazek 4crb; John Braid 34-5; Bukki88 120tl; Tomáš Bureš 2tr, 36-7; Valeria Cantone 4cr; Richie Chan 26br; Cphotography 57t; Dbeatson 34crb Elxeneize 6cla, 24-5, 26-7; Eudaemon 66t; Nicola Ferrari 71ca; Paula Fisher 132tr; Georgesixth 77clb; Giuseppemasci 94bl; Grian12 99tl; Nataliya Hora 49t; Irinadobrohotova63 65tr; Julietphotography 22c, 76cra; Holger Karius 126b; Andrea La Corte 13tr; Lowsun 6ca, 117tl; Thomas Lukassek 44crb; Douglas Mackenzie 108tl; Magsellen 85tr; Daniel Masters 103b; James Mcquarrie 26cb; Meunierd 23c, 96tl; Jaroslaw Moravcik 48t; Photographerlondon 55bl; Photoprofi30 66bl; Photowitch 124-5bl; Pitsch22 90tr; Adrian Pluskota 4cl; Juergen Schonnop 32-3; Stevewphoto 30br; Yvonne Stewart 103tr; Stockcube 4cla; Sueburtonphotography 123t; Petr Švec 12-3, 28cl; Tazufos 31clb; Tonythomas1958 82-3; T.w. Van Urk 56cl; Stefano Valeri 91b; Andrew Ward 122br; Weetoonpics 122tl; Ketsiree Wongwan 19tl; Ian Woolcock 58t.

Edinburgh Festival Fringe Society: Jane Barlow 69cl.

Eilean Donan Castle: 41t.

Fife Coast and Countryside Trust: Richard Newton 53clb.

Getty Images: AFP/Andy Buchanan 39bl; Alan Copson 3tl, 72-3; Ross Gilmore 68tr; Maremagnum 3tr, 44-5, 134-5; Michael Breitung Photography 114-5; Oxford Science Archive/Print Collector 39cla; David C Tomlinson 15ca; Adina Tovy 43tr.

Glamis Castle: 42tl 93clb.

Go Ape: Red Consultancy 60tl.

Inveraray Castle: 105bl.

Isle of Eriska: Dennis Hardley Photography 71crb.

iStockphoto.com: jewhyte 79tr.

Knockinaam Lodge: 65cl, 89br.

Landmark Forest Adventure Park: Captivating Photography/Charné Hawkes 61t.

Loch Lomond & The Trossachs National Park: 52t.

Mary Evans Picture Library: Illustration by J R Skelton in Scotland's Story (1906) 38tl.

Moonfish Cafe: 113c.

National Galleries Of Scotland: Van Gogh, Orchard in Blossom 17bl.

National Museums of Scotland: 18bc; Stewart Attwood 18cr.

National Trust for Scotland: Arduaine Garden 33cra; Kathy Collins 33bc; John Sinclair 32bl, 112bl.

Princes Square: 100br.

Scarista House: 127cra.

Scottish National Galleries: Lady Agnew of Lochnaw (1932) by John Singer Sargent 16tr.

Scottish National Gallery of Modern Art: 77tl.

Scottish National Heritage: Becky Duncan Photography 53br.

Scottish Seabird Centre: 61cb.

The Achiltibuie Garden Ltd: Allan Graham 49tr.

The Dome: 80bl.

The Kitchin: 81c.

The Peat Inn: Cill Mair 64cb, 95tr.

The Witchery by the Castle: 64t.

Cover
Front & spine: **AWL Images:** Tom Mackie.
Back: **123RF.com:** Jacek Nowak crb, stroop ll; **AWL Images:** Tom Mackie b; **Dreamstime.com:** Leonid Andronov cla, Helen Hotson tr.

Pull Out Map Cover
AWL Images: Tom Mackie.

All other images © Dorling Kindersley
For further information see: www.dkimages.com

As a guide to abbreviations in visitor information blocks: **Adm** = admission charge; **D** = dinner; **L** = lunch.

Penguin Random House

Printed and bound in China

First edition in 2003

Published in Great Britain
by Dorling Kindersley Limited
80 Strand, London WC2R 0RL

Published in the United States by
DK Publishing, 1450 Broadway, Suite 801,
New York, NY 10018, USA

A CIP catalogue record is available from the British Library.

A catalog record for this book is available from the Library of Congress.

ISSN 1479-344X

ISBN 978-0-2414-0872-8

SPECIAL EDITIONS OF DK TRAVEL GUIDES

DK Travel Guides can be purchased in bulk quantities at discounted prices for use in promotions or as premiums. We also offer special editions and personalized jackets, corporate imprints, and excerpts from all our books, tailored specifically to meet your needs.

To find out more, please contact:

in the US
specialsales@dk.com
in the UK
travelguides@uk.dk.com
in Canada
specialmarkets@dk.com
in Australia
**penguincorporatesales@
penguinrandomhouse.com.au**

MIX
Paper from responsible sources
FSC™ C018179
FSC www.fsc.org

Selected Street Index